1969 £4-0

COMMON PRAYER
IN THE
CHURCH OF ENGLAND

COMMON PRAYER
IN THE
CHURCH OF ENGLAND

By

D. E. W. HARRISON

Dean of Bristol

LONDON

S · P · C · K

1969

First published as The Book of Common Prayer
by the Canterbury Press in 1946
Reprinted 1959, with corrections, and in 1962
by S.P.C.K.
Revised edition with new title, 1969
S.P.C.K.
Holy Trinity Church, Marylebone Road, London N.W.1.
Made and printed by offset in Great Britain by
William Clowes and Sons, Limited, London and Beccles

SBN 281 02341 7

Preface

MUCH has happened since this little book was first published in 1946 and, in a revised edition, in 1959. The Church of England has entered a period of liturgical experiment, based on documents prepared by a liturgical commission appointed by the Archbishops; the Church of Rome is not only revising its liturgy but has accepted the Reformation principle of using the vernacular; a Joint Liturgical Group of English and Scottish liturgists of the main denominations testifies to the common concern for liturgical reform and has published proposals for a daily office and for a eucharistic lectionary. The attempt has therefore been made to incorporate in this new edition the material relevant to Prayer Book revision. The first five chapters remain unchanged, since the background of worship in the early and medieval Church is still relevant to the understanding of the Reformation changes, but the remainder of the book has been extensively revised. My hope is still that expressed in the foreword of the first edition: "If this book enables English churchmen the better to understand the greatness of their heritage, it will have achieved its object."

Bristol, 1969   D. E. W. HARRISON

Contents

PREFACE   v

PART ONE
Christian Worship

1 Fundamentals   3
2 Christian Worship in the Early Church   13
3 Worship in the Medieval Church   25
4 Worship and the Reformation   35
5 The Making of the Prayer Book, 1549–1662   45
6 The Background of Liturgical Change, 1662–1965   56

PART TWO
The Contents of the English Prayer Book

7   The Holy Communion   65
8   The Daily Services and Litany   82
9   The Occasional Offices   97
10 The Ordinal   110
11 The Future of Prayer Book Revision   119

PART THREE
Notes

1 The Early Liturgies   127
2 The Daily Offices of the Sarum Breviary   128
3 The Black Rubric   129
4 The Homilies   129

INDEX   131

PART ONE

CHRISTIAN WORSHIP

1

Fundamentals

In the New Testament worship is seldom defined, but always taken for granted. The Gospels leave us with the disciples continually in the Temple blessing God; the Temple was the place where the early Church was naturally to be found. This is important because it is evidence of the fact that the first Christian community possessed from its very beginning a heritage of praise and prayer, the worship of the Church of the Old Testament. If, in one sense, the Christian Church began with Peter's confession of our Lord's Messiahship, and in another with the gift of the Spirit at Pentecost, it is also true that through our Lord it claimed continuity with that Church of God which began with the call of Abraham. It claimed as its own the Old Testament scriptures, for pre-eminently they bore witness to Christ the Lord of the Church; it could and did use, with deepened understanding, Jewish forms of prayer and praise, finding, more especially in the Psalms, Christianly understood, a treasury of devotion. The worship of the synagogue, which Jesus himself had shared, remained as the ante-chapel of the worship of the Christian Church. All this can be put another way by saying that worship is dependent upon revelation, upon God's self-disclosure of his own nature and purpose; and therefore the Old Testament is not superseded but fully used, because in Christ its partially-veiled meaning has now been disclosed.

Important as this is, it is, however, only part of the truth. The new wine of the Gospel could not be contained in the old wineskins of Judaism; the Spirit could not be confined to the letter; the Christian experience, with its dominant note of joy and freedom, its consciousness of being not under law but under grace, was bound to transcend, in its expression in worship, the rigid forms of the synagogue. The picture painted for us in 1 Corinthians of the worship of the Church at Corinth, with its prophecy and speaking with tongues, has not untruly been called the liturgy of the Spirit. It had its dangers, as St Paul clearly knew, but, nevertheless, as he also recognized, it was a real expression of the work of the Holy Spirit in the hearts of men; and in later ages Christians of the Reformed Churches have rightly claimed a like freedom in worship, the freedom of the Spirit. Worship, if it is to be Christian, is essentially "worship in spirit", as our Lord told the woman of Samaria. The content of this freedom needs, however, to be carefully safeguarded from misunderstanding. What is true of St Paul's epistles in the realm of Christian doctrine is true in a precisely parallel sense of Christian worship. On the one hand, epistles like Galatians and Romans have, as their dominant theme, Christian liberty. On the other, the Corinthian letters insist that this liberty is not licence. The Spirit is the Spirit of Christ, the one, holy, Spirit of God, and therefore there is an inner constraint of the Spirit producing harmony and order.

Now at a deeper level this implies that Christian worship is subject always to a theological constraint which is also the constraint of the Spirit. The Spirit's work is defined in St John's Gospel as taking the things of Christ and showing them unto us. Worship is dependent upon revelation, and Christian worship is dependent upon the revelation of God in Christ. This is the meaning of the full-orbed definition which our Lord gives us when he speaks of "worship in spirit and in truth". It must be worship of the one true God, and therefore its very heart must be the setting forth of the saving acts of God by which he has made himself known to men. The "Word of God" must first be proclaimed before the true response of the worshippers can be called forth. The Gospel must be announced if men are truly to give glory to God. The Old Testament commandment, quoted by our Lord himself, is basic also in the New. "Thou shalt worship the Lord thy God, and him only shalt thou serve." And this one true God is now for all time the God and Father of our Lord Jesus Christ. The place of apprehension from which worship must spring is "the word made flesh"; for "the Word", the pure expression of the Being and Will of God, "became flesh and tabernacled amongst us,

4

and we beheld his glory, the glory as of the only-begotten of the Father, full of grace and truth".

This theological basis of Christian worship can be illustrated again and again from the New Testament itself. In the writings of St John, Christian life and worship alike are "controlled" by the "flesh of Jesus". Not every spirit is to be believed. "Hereby know ye the Spirit of God: Every spirit that confesseth not that Jesus is come in the flesh is not of God."[1] The same truth is significantly set out in the Gospel at the very beginning of our Lord's ministry. Our Lord cleansed the Temple, proclaiming by his act the imperfection of Old Testament worship, and when challenged replied, "Destroy this temple, and in three days I will raise it up." "He spake", says St John, "of the Temple of his Body." The Body of Jesus, his flesh, was the tabernacle of the Word, the abiding place of the Spirit, the shrine of the presence of God.[2] So, in the great discourse on the Bread of Life in Chapter 6, the true bread is "my flesh which I will give for the life of the world", and the words which Jesus speaks are "spirit and life". Similarly, in St Paul's epistles and notably in Ephesians the whole teaching of the Apostle, and more particularly his praise and prayer, spring from his contemplation of the saving purpose of God in and through Jesus Christ. Ephesians 1.15–22 is St Paul's response to the grace of God whose glory he has sung in the first fourteen verses. So again 1 Peter begins with the blessing of God for all that he has done for his people, for what we may quite simply call the Gospel. Everything which follows is Christian response. It is not enough, then, to say that worship is free. In one sense only is that true; if the freedom is the freedom of the Spirit: the Spirit bearing witness to Christ, the Christ who is the Word made flesh, in whom dwelleth all the fullness of the Godhead bodily. The Church came to see that this freedom must be safeguarded.

The simplest of all safeguards, the most flexible, but not the surest, is the character of the Christian minister, for quite clearly, from what has already been said, worship must be set in the context of the ministry of the Word, and ministry implies a minister. It is now widely recognized that ministry grew up within the Apostolic Church to meet the Church's growing needs. The Apostle was there from the beginning, but prophets and teachers, presbyters and deacons

[1] 1 John 4.2.   [2] Hoskyns, *The Fourth Gospel*, p. 207.

5

soon followed. All, in some sense, were ministers of the Word. St Paul, indeed, could wish that all Christians were prophets[1] subject only to the essential safeguard of the confession "Jesus is Lord". Revelation, knowledge, prophesying, doctrine were all modes of the Word of God, and linked in the ministry of the Spirit's gifts. But those gifts and the ministries corresponding to them were not individualistic. Their context was the life of the one body which grew in response to them. There was a *consensus fidelium*, a common Christian faith known to all through the apostolic ministry, which was itself a safeguard. It was this faith of the Church which could be relied upon as a bulwark against error. It was the Christian discipline of the whole body which was in great measure trusted to exclude false teachers. This primary safeguard of the truth must be mentioned because it was not only practised in the primitive Church but in modern times has sometimes been regarded as the only criterion of the Christian ministry of the Word. We must, however, go on to set beside it a second, which historically has been of great importance, and which may be called the principle of liturgy.

Liturgy meant originally the discharge of a public office, the service of the Greek city-state, by a private citizen; but in the Greek translation of the O.T., the Septuagint, it had been used of the priestly service of God discharged by the Levitical priesthood on behalf of all Israel the People of God. The word comes thus to be used in the Christian Church of the worship and service of God, and in a specialized sense of the Holy Communion or Eucharist. From the very beginning the life of the Christian Church centred round the Apostles' doctrine, the fellowship, the breaking of bread and the prayers. The Word of God has already been seen to be the context of true worship. The fellowship of God's people within which and to which it is spoken has been seen to be an essential safeguard. What must now be taken seriously is the central importance of the "breaking of bread" with its origin in the rite of the Upper Room. There, in St John's phrase, Jesus sanctified himself, separated himself for sacrifice. There he expressed the meaning of his sacrificial death in bread broken and wine outpoured. There he himself gave the symbols of his Passion to his disciples that in prophetic symbolism—that is, in reality—they might share his Passion, feeding on the Bread of Life,

[1] 1 Cor. 14.5.

6

eating his flesh and drinking his blood. What is enshrined in the Lord's Supper is therefore the heart of the gospel; nowhere in the Gospels is the meaning of Christ's death so clearly set forth as in the words and actions of the Upper Room. It is indeed almost impossible to over-exaggerate the importance of this rite, and, we may add, of the other Dominical sacrament of Baptism. "The truth", says Denney, "seems to be that both the sacraments are forms into which we may put as much of the Gospel as they will carry; and St Paul, for his part, practically puts the whole of his gospel into each."[1] So again St John, at the close of the first Christian century, when he speaks of the water and the blood as "bearing witness in earth"[2] is clearly thinking of the Christian sacraments as witnesses to the historical reality of the life and work of our Lord. Moreover in his gospel he has given us clear exposition of the meaning of Baptism and the Lord's supper in his third and sixth chapters, and once again the inference is indisputable; the sacraments enshrined the heart of the Gospel. But if the two Dominical rites are on the same level as sacraments of the Gospel, as indeed they are, it was also inevitable that the rite of the Supper should come to have a pre-eminent place in the worship of the Church just because it was the service of every Lord's day. Christian worship is pre-eminently that proclaiming of the Lord's death till he come, which has its focus in the breaking of bread and the sharing of the one cup. Here, according to his own word, the Risen Lord, the Lamb as it had been slain, was present with his own. Here, truly, he was known of them in the breaking of bread.

It is round the Eucharist, therefore, that Christian devotion gathered. Here in spoken word the saving Gospel was proclaimed; here the scriptures, first of the Old and later of the New Testament, were expounded; here the Psalms of the Old Dispensation and the hymns of the New proclaimed the reconciling love of God in Christ; here, in fellowship, reconciled to God and to one another through the death of his Son, Christians both expressed their fellowship and found it renewed and deepened as they partook of that one Bread. It was thus that the Gospel of the holy reconciling love of God was set at the heart of Christian worship in a service for sinful men, yet called to be saints. It was in this way that witness was borne to the saving acts of God reaching their consummation in the Cross and the

---

[1] *The Death of Christ*, p. 137.   [2] 1 John 5.8.

Resurrection and the gift of the Spirit. It was from the Table of the Lord that Christians went out, renewed in spirit from the presence of their Risen Master, to live and witness for him as the Church, which is his body.

At first all this was in great measure, judging by what evidence we possess, without fixed form. The essential principle of liturgy is not the use of set forms but the setting forth of the saving acts of God, and, above all else, of the Cross of Christ. An extension of the same fundamental principle has brought into being the Christian year. That year is built round the cardinal points of the life of our Lord; Christmas commemorates his birth, Epiphany his baptism and universal mission, Passiontide and Easter his death and resurrection, Whitsuntide the gift of his Spirit. It is thus that, one by one, the acts of God in Christ for men become in turn the special emphasis of the Church's worship; yet always they are set within the framework of his whole life and the perfection of his saving work. In the course of the centuries extempore prayer gave place to set forms, and both chants and ceremonial became increasingly elaborate, but in its essentials the service remained the same, and the worship was worship in the truth.

Worship then is in spirit and it is in truth, and both elements are essential. The danger is that in emphasizing one aspect the other is lost sight of, or at least minimized. The English Church inherits a liturgical tradition. Worship in truth is therefore safeguarded in so far as the forms of prayer and praise truly embody God's revelation of himself. What is in danger of being forgotten is that this same worship must also be in Spirit; which means that man's offering of worship is itself conditioned by the prior activity of the Spirit of God himself. No recital of what God has done for man will ever move him to the only true response, the spiritual worship of the offering of soul and body to God afresh, unless it "comes home" to man; and only God by his Spirit can make that happen. No human words of Liturgy or Bible or preacher can in themselves convert a soul: that, God must do. No worship is real which is an attempt by man to lift himself to God: it is God who must lift him. St Paul reminds the Corinthians that where worship is real, the outsider coming in will confess that God is with them, and so will himself be led to worship. In the final analysis this means that the use even of the most perfect

8

liturgical forms will not save a Church from being dead. Unless the Church is at least in some measure the realized fellowship of the Spirit, unless its worship includes expectant faith in the activity of the Spirit, its worship may be aesthetically and even doctrinally perfect, but it will not be alive.

Once again, this is only the working out in terms of worship of Christian doctrine. Christian living is faith in response to God's grace, in response, that is, to the present self-giving of God: one with the gift of Calvary, perfectly manifested in an event of history, but nevertheless present, personal activity. Christian living is surrender, self-oblation in response to the reconciling love of God which seeks men here and now. Grace and faith, love and grateful response, these together constitute our communion with God, but at every point faith is dependent upon grace, our love for God upon his love for us. So, too, Christian worship is essentially response, but response not merely or even primarily to the revelation of God in history, but to that revelation brought near and made for us present reality in the power of the Spirit. So in one of the earliest liturgies, that of the eighth book of the Apostolic Constitutions, God is asked to send his Spirit and "show this bread to be the Body of Christ and the Cup his Blood". The Spirit is to take the things of Christ and show them to the worshippers.

There is, however, another approach to the understanding of worship which also has its roots in the New Testament. St Paul in Romans 8.26, speaks of the Spirit as helping our infirmities "for we know not what we should pray for as we ought, but the Spirit himself maketh intercession for us". With this may be linked the title of Paraclete in St John's Gospel which may mean advocate or intercessor as well as helper or strengthener. Similarly our Lord's intercession for us is common to the thought of St Paul and the writer of the Epistle to the Hebrews. For the latter it is the continuing activity of Christ as High Priest. "He ever liveth to make intercession for us." Worship therefore consists in being united with Christ by the Spirit in that offering of himself to God which on Calvary was the fulfilment and consummation of all sacrifice. It means being made one with the only perfect response to the love of God, the complete self-giving in love and obedience of our Lord to his Father. It is "being accepted in the beloved". It is only "in Him" that we are made acceptable to the Father, given our place in the new humanity, the new Israel, a holy priesthood, to offer up spiritual sacrifices acceptable to God through Jesus Christ. Worship, therefore, is rightly understood as the Church's sacrifice, the offering of herself in union with her Lord, and on this foundation the "catholic" theory of worship has come to rest. In the course of the Middle Ages, however, it was distorted. The offering became the offering of Christ by the Church as propitiating the Father, and the essential element of faith-union with our Lord was obscured. In the New Testament, however, the work of our Lord is itself the embodiment of the love of the Father, "God was in Christ reconciling the world to himself", and St John is equally insistent on this truth. "At that day ye shall ask in my name: and I say not unto you that I will pray the Father for you: for the Father himself loveth you because ye have loved me, and have believed that I came out from God." It is for this reason that the Churches of the Reformation, convinced in Calvin's phrase that believers "have the heart of God", have found it necessary to safe-guard their worship from what they rightly regarded as serious error. The fact that in our own Anglican Communion service the prayer of oblation follows communion is neither a historical accident nor of negligible doctrinal importance. Rather it marks the essential character of that service as reformed. We offer ourselves because we have first received the Body and Blood of Christ; we present our bodies a living sacrifice enabled by God's self-giving to us.

Worship then is in spirit and in truth. But it is also, and essentially, the worship of the Church, of the whole Church in heaven and in earth. It is "with Angels and Archangels and all the company of heaven" that we say "Holy, Holy, Holy, Glory be to thee, O Lord most high." The Church is the family of God, The Body of Christ, The Temple of God's Spirit. In any one place it may be represented only by a tiny company, two or three gathered together in Christ's name; but the Lord of the whole Church by his Spirit is in the midst, and worship becomes possible. This, in the New Testament, is perfectly clear. Our Lord's preaching was of the Kingdom of God, and despite some modern writers Kingdom means more than sovereignty; it means a realm of sovereignty: it implies the coming into being of a people of God. Therefore, Jesus taught men to pray "*Our* Father", and spoke of a Church which explicitly in Matthew 16.18, and implicitly in Matthew 18.17 is *his* church in distinction from the old *ecclesia* of Israel. The disciples are all brethren, sons of one Father; all are united to himself so that what men do to them is counted as done to him. Here, then, in the Gospels are the root conceptions which in developed form give us the New Testament doctrine of the Church. Perhaps the most striking passage is 1 Corinthians 12.12, "For as the body is one, and hath many members, and all the members of that one body, being many, are one body: so also is Christ. For by one Spirit are we all baptized into one body": on which Calvin commented, "He calls Christ the church." So using another metaphor, that of the bride of Christ, St Paul can write in Ephesians 5.25, "Christ loved the church and gave himself for it." With this background of thought, common to St Paul, St Peter, and St John, it is not surprising to find that Christian worship is everywhere conceived as corporate. It is the worship of the family, of one Body, one with Christ its Head through the Spirit, dependent upon him continually for its very life, continuously being built up in love to the praise of God's glory. Just as St Paul does not think even of the faith-relationship to Christ as a purely individual experience, but insists that it is "with all saints" that we are able to know "what is the breadth and length and depth and height and to know the love of Christ which passeth knowledge", so he goes on to insist that it is "in the church and in Christ Jesus" that glory is given to God. So, to pass outside the New Testament, the earliest liturgies are full of the sense that the worship of the Lord's Table is the worship of the Church. At every stage of the service the congregation is reminded that what is being said is in their name, that they, through the ministers, really share in every stage of the offering to God of the sacrifice of praise and thanksgiving. As St Augustine reminded his catechumens, "The mystery of yourselves is laid upon the altar."

Finally, worship is the one true preparation of the Church as the Body of Christ for its work in the world which is to be the Body of Christ, the instrument which our Lord uses to carry forward his purposes for men. "What we become in the presence of God", says an old German mystic, "that we can be all day long." It is through worship that the Church becomes more firmly united to Christ her head; more fitted, therefore, to do his work. Worship and witness are interdependent. Just as in the New Testament solitary worship is confined to the forced isolation of a John on Patmos, so solitary witness may be forced on a Christian, but is not the unified witness to the world for which our Lord prayed in the Upper Room. The ideal for the Church is that picture of its activity which meets us in the opening pages of the Acts. The Church gathered together in prayer and praise empowered by the Spirit goes out to witness to men, proclaiming in word and life the saving Gospel by which it lives. Just as in worship there is a priesthood of all believers, so also in witness the Church has a priestly Ministry which all its members share. "Mine", says St Paul, "is a priestly ministry of Jesus Christ, ministering as a priest the Gospel of God, that the sacrificial offering of the Gentiles might be acceptable, being sanctified by the Holy Spirit" (Rom. 15.16). That is a ministry which belongs to every Christian, but to every Christian as a member of the royal priesthood, the Church of God. So at the close of Christian worship in the English Church we pray "that we may do all such good works as God has prepared for us to walk in". Worship which is real makes us more fit for life, and that is always its ultimate test. "By their fruits ye shall know them." What matters is not whether worship makes us feel good or happy; what matters is whether it makes us Christ-like; whether men take knowledge of us that we have been with Jesus.

2

Christian Worship in the Early Church

THE first three centuries of the Christian era are the age of persecution. Christianity was a forbidden religion and though persecution was by no means continuous it is not surprising that liturgical books, even if they existed, have not survived. The most sacred of Christian rites, the Lord's Supper, was, moreover, carefully guarded. Only the faithful were present; even the catechumens, though candidates for baptism, were admitted only to the first part of the service. Our information is therefore scanty. For the second century we have two descriptions of Christian worship, one by a pagan in Pliny's letter to Trajan (A.D. 112), one by a Christian, Justin Martyr (c. A.D. 140). In Clement of Rome's letter to the Corinthians at the close of the first century there is a long and beautiful prayer which we may take as typical of the celebrant's great intercession at the Lord's Supper; and in addition a document called the *Didaché* or Teaching of the Twelve Apostles, the date of which is still uncertain (possibly c. 130–40), gives us forms of prayer, markedly Jewish in character but including thanksgiving for the cup and the loaf. For the third century we have the writings of Clement of Alexandria, Tertullian, Origen, Cyprian and, of great interest, the book called *The Egyptian Church Order* which is substantially a translation of *The Apostolic Tradition* written in Greek by Hippolytus of Rome shortly before A.D. 250. This contains the earliest known consecration prayer. For the fourth century we have the prayer book of Sarapion, Bishop of Thmuis in the Nile Delta (c. A.D. 340), and at the end of the century our first complete liturgy in the eighth book of the *Apostolic Constitutions*. Information from Christian writers then becomes more abundant and we can give a fairly complete account of Christian worship except, strange though it is, that of the Roman Church.

There is no space in what is only intended as an introduction to the Prayer Book to consider these sources in detail; a general outline must suffice. First it is clear that the worship of the Christian Church owes much to the Synagogue; and the backbone of Synagogue worship was the reading of the Old Testament scriptures. These were commented upon and expounded. Our Lord expounded Isaiah in the synagogue of Nazareth, and St Paul spoke freely in the synagogues of the Dispersion. The Psalms were certainly used and possibly, though not certainly, sung; what was in effect the Creed of Judaism, the Shema (Deut. 6.4–9; 11.13–21, Num. 15.37–41), was recited together with the Benedictions, which are in effect prayers and thanksgivings to which the congregation said Amen. To this extent the service of the Synagogue was liturgical in structure, and by the beginning of the second century the Benedictions were in fixed form. The rabbis, however, were averse from fixed forms of prayer and extempore prayer was certainly normal in the early Christian Church. The *Didaché* insists that at the Eucharist or Love-feast (the precise nature of the service is not clear) the prophets are to be allowed to give thanks as they wish. Justin Martyr says that at the Eucharist the President gives thanks "according to his ability"; and as late as Hippolytus, though a fixed form is provided, it is not prescribed. The celebrant still has liberty to pray extempore "according to his own ability". It is not until the end of the fourth century that fixed forms are normal, and even later the introduction of new prayers took place in the non-Roman West.

Against this background we can set what we know of second-century Christian worship. The only congregational services were those of Sunday. The Christian inherited from Judaism the practice of prayer three times a day, and the *Didaché* directs that the Lord's Prayer shall thus be used. The third, sixth, and ninth hours are assumed to be the hours of prayer by the end of the century, and prayer during the night is recommended. Fasting, too, is a similar inheritance from Judaism; Wednesdays and Fridays being observed as fasts. But on Sundays Christians met twice. First, before daybreak, according to Pliny, they met to sing a hymn to Christ as God, and bound themselves by an oath (*sacramentum*) to abstain from evil. Later they met again for a common and harmless meal. This piece of evidence may be variously interpreted. *Sacramentum* may have been misunderstood by a pagan. It might refer to the Lord's Supper, the later meal being the *Agapé* or Love-feast. Alternatively the first service may have been an early form of morning prayer (Lauds) and the later service the Eucharist. We have, however, a description of the Christian Eucharist in Justin Martyr which by comparison with later accounts we can see to be typical.

The service begins with readings from the prophets and "the memoirs of the apostles [that is to say the Gospels] for as long as time permits. Then, when the reader has ended, the President instructs and encourages the people to practise the truths contained in the scripture lections. Thereafter, we all stand up and offer prayers together." Thus far we have a Christian version of the Synagogue service, for although Justin does not mention Psalms, it is almost certain that they were already in use. Dr Maxwell suggests for this first part of the service the apt title "The liturgy of the Word".

Then comes the kiss of peace, and "bread, and a cup of wine mixed with water, are brought to the President". (At this point a collection of gifts was made for the poor; for although Justin himself does not specify the exact place of this collection in the service we can supply it from later evidence.) This is the offertory—the sacrifice which Christians can offer to God of his own gifts. "Then the President offers up prayers and thanksgivings, according to his ability, and the people cry aloud, saying Amen. Each one then receives a portion and share of the Elements over which thanks have been given; and which are also carried and ministered by the deacons to those absent." Justin adds that "this food is called by us Eucharist, of which it is not right for anyone to partake save only he who believes that the things taught by us are true, and is washed with the washing that is for forgiveness of sins and regeneration, and lives as Christ commanded us". The liturgy of the Word is thus followed by the liturgy of the Upper Room.

Here, then, is the outline which, though filled out and enriched, has remained substantially the same through the centuries, and can be recognized in the English Book of Common Prayer. The *Sanctus* certainly goes back to the early years of the third century, when we have evidence for its use in Alexandria; and a little later Cyprian mentions the *Sursum Corda*—"lift up your hearts", which in subsequent liturgies, as in our own, introduces the prayer of consecration. Equally ancient is the Salutation, "The Lord be with you", with the response, "and with thy spirit": while the invitation, "Let us give thanks to our Lord God", was inherited by the Church from Jewish usage.

With Hippolytus we reach the first extant consecration prayer. Its structure is simple. It begins with THANKSGIVING to the Father, through Jesus Christ, sent for our salvation, the Word of God, who became man, who came to suffer that he might destroy death, break the fetters of the devil, illuminate the righteous, and manifest the resurrection, who took bread and cup adding, "Do this in remembrance of me".

Then follows the OFFERING or OBLATION. "Wherefore, mindful of his death and resurrection we offer thee this bread and cup, giving thee thanks."

Then the INVOCATION or *Epiklesis*. "And we pray thee that (thou wouldest send thy Holy Spirit upon the oblation of thy holy church, that)[1] thou wouldest grant to all who partake to be made one, that they may be fulfilled with Holy Spirit for the confirmation of faith in truth." The Prayer closes with a doxology and the people's Amen.

Here also is a structure which expanded, enriched, and sometimes distorted is found in all the later liturgies, though most clearly in the East. The heart of the service is a Thanksgiving: there is no formula by which the elements are consecrated. It is only later, and then only in the West, that the words of institution of the Upper Room are regarded as in themselves consecrating, or setting apart, the elements for their sacramental use. The primitive approach is clear. The words of the Lord are the authority for what the Church does: for what she receives she is dependent upon the act of God through the Spirit for which she prays. The importance of this distinction will become clear as we study the making of our own Prayer Book, but here in Hippolytus we have the mind of the early Church over a century before our earliest complete liturgy.

[1] The words in brackets are probably a later addition to the text. In the developed Eastern rite this Invocation of the Spirit on the oblation was regarded as fundamentally important.

16

With the *Apostolic Constitutions* (*c.* A.D. 375) we reach a complete (Syrian) liturgy which may, for our purposes, represent the East, though it has many features peculiar to itself. The service which this document implies has often been described[1] and is here outlined. The service begins with Bible lections—a series from the Old Testament, Epistles, Acts, Gospels, the Gospel being given special honour, with the congregation standing to hear it. Between the lections come the Psalms. The sermons follow, each priest present having the right to preach, the bishop coming last. The deacon then begins the litany for the catechumens and penitents, who depart in turn with a blessing from the bishop, till only the faithful remain.

The deacon now begins the litany of the faithful, the congregation replying to each petition *Kyrie eleison*: Lord, have mercy. The bishop's long prayer of intercession follows. This brings the liturgy of the Word, which the Church took over from the Synagogue, to an end.

The liturgy of the Upper Room then begins with the bishop's salutation followed by the kiss of peace. The doors are watched to exclude all but the faithful, the bread and wine and the gifts of the congregation are solemnly offered, and the clergy gather round the bishop at the table of the Lord. After the grace and the *Sursum Corda* comes what now would be called The Preface, the recitation of all the saving acts of God beginning from the Creation, commemorating God's choice of a people and his mighty acts on their behalf. Into this breaks the *Sanctus*—sung by the whole congregation, and in the solemn stillness which follows the eucharistic prayer goes on to commemorate the work of our Lord, his incarnation, life and passion, reciting the narrative of the institution, and calling to remembrance not only his death but his resurrection, his ascension and the hope of his return in glory. Finally the bishop prays that the Holy Spirit will descend upon the gifts offered according to the Lord's command that they may be shown to be Body and Blood of Christ and the spiritual food of his faithful people. The Prayer of consecration proper is ended, but the bishop goes on to the great intercession for all sorts and conditions of men, ending with the doxology and the people's Amen.

Then comes communion, with the beautiful invitation, "Holy

[1] E.g. Duchesne: *Christian Worship*, p. 57 f.

things for holy people." To each communicant the bishop said, "The Body of Christ", to which the response was Amen. The deacon who administered the cup said, "The Blood of Christ, chalice of life". During communion a psalm was sung and the service ended with a prayer, a final blessing, and the deacon's bidding, "Depart in peace".

This account must suffice as a description of a service of Holy Communion in the East at the end of the fourth century, though all the evidence points to a wide variety of primitive usage which only later became standardized. Local churches influenced one another and the liturgy was shaped by a constant process of borrowing and adaptation. What is true of the East is apparently true of the West also.[1] Liturgists speak of Italian rites of which the Roman is one, and of Gallican rites found in Spain, France, and probably Britain. Here too we can trace a process of growth of revision, though the early history of the Roman rite is still obscure. But when we compare the final development of the liturgy as represented in the West by Rome and in the East by Byzantium there are broad differences which are important for us, because our English Prayer Book remains essentially a revision and simplification of the Roman rite, and so, however briefly, they must be considered.[2]

The East is mystical, the West practical. The East loves to contemplate the being of God, the West his activity. The difference comes out well in a comparison of the Apostles' creed, which is based on the old Roman creed, and is content to state facts, with the Nicene creed, which is Eastern in origin and is much more theological. The East therefore thinks in terms of revelation, of mystery revealed. So our Lord's life is essentially manifestation, the showing to men of what is eternally true, and this manifestation is continued in the Church by the work of the Holy Spirit. The West, on the other hand, thinks of what Christ has done for man. It therefore concentrates on the thought of the efficacy of his death, shown forth till he come in sacrifice commemorated. So again the final emphasis of the East is upon the mystery of the resurrection and true life, immortality, made available to men through their union with the risen humanity of our Lord. The West concentrates all its thoughts upon Calvary,

[1] See Note 1.
[2] See F. Gavin's article, "The Eucharist in East and West", in *Liturgy and Worship*.

and the heart of the rite is receiving the benefits of that passion of the Lord which the rite sets forth. To these fundamentally important theological differences others of great interest may be added. The Eastern prayers are much longer, richer and fuller, but they tend also to become not only theological but ornate and rhetorical, ending in long and beautiful doxologies. In the West the terseness of the Latin kept prayers shorter, compact, condensed; the style familiar to us in the daily collects which are direct translations from the original Latin.

Finally we may notice that the Calendar affects the rite in the East and West respectively in different ways. In the East the consecration prayer itself changes with the season, whereas in the West it is virtually unchanged throughout the year. But apart from the consecration prayer, it is the Roman liturgy which was more profoundly influenced by the Christian year. Not only the lections but the prayers and the chants changed from week to week. This is hidden from us because in Cranmer's simplification of the Latin rite for English use it was precisely this rich variation which was cut away. Probably few Englishmen would, however, sacrifice the simplicity which now is ours.

Before we leave the service of Holy Communion in the early Church two simple facts may be mentioned which in view of later developments are not only interesting but important. First, it is worth remembering that the primitive position of the celebrant was facing the people. Churches were normally basilicas with a western apse. The clergy sat round the apse with the bishop's seat in the centre. The altar, or holy table, was roughly on the chord of the apse, and raised above the level of the congregation. The mosaics at Ravenna illustrate this ancient use, and the conservatism of Rome retains it when the Pope celebrates in his cathedral of St John Lateran. It is only later, when the altar was closely related to the saint's shrine, that the position of the celebrant was changed so that, together with the congregation, he faced the shrine. Even so, the primitive position was retained in some places, as for example in the Norman Cathedral of Norwich. The other significant fact is that in the East the element of mystery was heightened by veiling the altar from the congregation during the celebration of the holy mysteries. This veil and its light screen developed into the solid "iconostasis" (so called because of its "icons" or sacred images), normally of stone, and pierced only by the holy doors. The action of the Lord's Supper now takes place wholly out of the sight and hearing of the congregation, which awaits the opening of the royal doors with expectant prayer.

There can be no shadow of doubt that the Eucharist was of supreme importance in the early Church, but then, as now, it did not stand alone. Some account must therefore be given of the historical antecedents of the other services of our English Prayer Book, and first of the other sacrament of the Gospel, Holy Baptism.

The New Testament evidence itself is not entirely clear. There is some evidence that in the earliest days baptism was in the name of Jesus, but St Matthew 28.19 makes it clear that the normal practice was baptism in the name of the Trinity. Again, normally, baptism was by immersion in rivers or streams, but there is early evidence that baptism by pouring water, by affusion, was allowed as an alternative. The meaning of the rite is explained by St Paul. It meant the sharing of Christ's death and resurrection, the assurance of forgiveness for the past and power for the future, and both through the power of the Holy Spirit. It meant also incorporation into Christ's Body, the Church, "for by one Spirit are we all baptized into one body". The Acts of the Apostles more than once connects this rite of baptism with the laying on of hands. The action was natural for it signified, as in the Old Testament, that unity with the Church which baptism inaugurated. There is no clear evidence that it was a necessary part of the rite, but we should regard it as normal, especially in view of later development. On the part of the candidate a confession of faith was required, as of the Ethiopian eunuch; and with high probability a promise to live according to Christ's teaching, for St Peter speaks of "the answer of a good conscience towards God" (1 Pet. 3.21).

For the history of the development of the service in the early Church we have ample material in the *Didaché*, Justin Martyr, Tertullian, the *Apostolic Tradition*, and the catechetical lectures of Cyril of Jerusalem. The rite in all its essentials was fully developed by the end of the second century, and for our purposes it is only the developed Western rite which need concern us. The differences from the East are, in any case, of no importance. Baptism normally took place on Easter Eve, but sometimes at Whitsuntide in the West and Epiphany in the East. Preparation for baptism was long and searching. Pagans often delayed even for years, since the crucial step once taken made them subject to the rigorous discipline of the Church. When they gave in their names they were admitted to the catechumenate, exorcised (for the Church still believed in demons), signed with the cross, and given salt as a symbol of their Christian vocation. They now attended instructions in Christian faith and practice, in the East daily, but according to the final rule of the West on seven days in Lent. At these scrutinies, as they were called, the unworthy could be rejected. The catechumen was taught the Creed, the Lord's Prayer, and the meaning of the Gospel. At the last scrutiny on Easter Eve the priest touched the lips and ears of the candidates with saliva (in earlier days it was with oil), the symbolism being derived from St John 9.6. Having been signed with the cross they stripped and were anointed on back and breast with exorcized oil, and then solemnly renounced the devil, his works, and his pomps with a threefold, "I renounce." Then in the words of the Creed each made his Christian profession.

Baptism itself took place at the solemn vigil of Easter. The lections for that service included the whole story of God's dealings with his people, the creation, the flood, the sacrifice of Isaac, the passage of the Red Sea, the vision of Ezekiel, the story of Jonah, and passages from Daniel and the prophets, culminating in the institution of the Passover: each lection being followed by a prayer and sometimes by a canticle. The bishop—at Rome the Pope—and the clergy then accompanied the candidates to the baptistry and the font was blessed. The sign of the Cross was made in the water and tapers were plunged into the font at the invocation of the Holy Ghost. The bishop then poured consecrated oil (chrism) into the water and stirred it. The baptism then began. The candidates, stripped, were presented and replied to the three questions, "Dost thou believe in God the Father? in Jesus Christ? in the Holy Spirit?" with a threefold, "I believe." They were then thrice immersed with the words, "I baptize thee in the name of the Father and of the Son and of the Holy Ghost." After baptism the candidates were anointed with chrism, put on new white garments with the assistance of their sponsors, and then in groups were brought before the bishop. The bishop stretched his hand over them (elsewhere in the West laid hands on them), invoked the Holy Spirit, and signed them on the forehead with chrism. They then received their Easter communion, followed by a drink, composed of

21

honey, water, and milk, symbolizing their entry into the promised land.

Primitively the bishop was the minister of the whole service, but later, owing to pressure of numbers, he was content to begin the baptismal service at the font, and then to retire to the church for what later became confirmation. Both in the East and the West, and especially when infant baptism became the norm, the bishop delegated baptism wholly to the priesthood. In the East he retained only the blessing of the chrism, confirmation with it being like baptism delegated. In the West he retained the whole confirmation rite. This meant, further, especially in the territorial dioceses beyond the Alps, that the interval between baptism and confirmation grew, and what had been two parts of one rite became separated first in time and then in doctrine until in the Middle Ages confirmation became recognized as a separate sacrament. Meanwhile the Church continued to treat infants as though they were adults, performing the admission to the catechumenate at the church door and prefixing the essential ceremonies of the scrutinies to the baptism itself. The only important change was that the godparents replied to the questions asked of the child.

Having now considered the administration of the two sacraments of the Gospel in the early Church we can turn to the origins of the daily offices represented in our Prayer Book by Morning and Evening Prayer. Those origins are in fact by no means clear. The truth would seem to be that they were a natural growth, having a two-fold origin.[1] They grew, in the first place, out of the practice of private prayer and reading of scripture. We have already seen that devout Christians prayed three times a day, and even at night. In the *Apostolic Tradition* of Hippolytus, which became extremely popular in the East, and became the basis of Church Orders, manuals for the guidance of the life of local churches, regulations are given about prayer. Every Christian is commanded to pray on rising in the morning, at the third and sixth hours, because of their association with the Passion, at the ninth hour, on going to bed, and in the middle of the night, for at midnight the bridegroom might come. In addition, there are directions for the supper of the congregations when the bishop gives thanks and provision for daily assembly in church for instruction. If

See E. C. Ratcliff's article, "The Choir Offices", in *Liturgy and Worship*.

attendance at these is not possible, then scripture must be read at home daily. All this is private; but where Tertullian was content to exhort, Hippolytus enjoins. As E. C. Ratcliff points out, it is but a short step from obligatory prayer at fixed times to common prayer in church at the same times. That the step was taken is proved by the *Apostolic Constitutions* (*c.* 375–400), where we find provision for two principal daily services, morning and evening, for which psalms and prayers are appointed, while the other hours are also observed by services in church. These would all be kept by the clergy and the laity who had the leisure. Further development came with the growth of monasticism and asceticism.

Primarily then, the daily services grew out of the practice of private prayer, but their content was, indirectly, derived from the worship of the synagogue. The gap in time is too big for us to suppose, as Archdeacon Freeman did, that there was direct dependence; but, as we have already seen, the liturgy of the Word (or Mass of the Catechumens) was the Christian development of synagogue worship, and this in turn must have influenced the daily services. What at least, is clear is that the backbone of those services in their developed form was the Psalter and the reading of scripture lections.

In the West, which alone concerns us, the Roman laity and secular clergy kept six hours of prayer: Vigil or Mattins at midnight, Lauds in the early morning, Terce, Sext, None (third, sixth, and ninth hours), and Vespers in the evening. What later were called "the little hours", Terce, Sext, and None, were said publicly only on Sundays and festivals. Benedict, the founder of Western monasticism, added, following Basil's Eastern Rules, Prime in the early morning and Compline at bed-time. In course of time the secular clergy fell in with St Benedict's Rule, and we get the fully developed Choir Office or Divine service, but the services themselves retained some of the characteristics of the old Roman hours.

As has already been said, the backbone of these services was the Psalter, said through once in the week; Psalm 119 being divided between "the little hours" and the rest between Mattins, Lauds, and Vespers. Scripture lections were almost confined to Mattins; hymns, many of them composed by St Ambrose, were sung at each service. Gregory the Great, himself a monk, did much to develop the musical character of the service, and soon the Roman Chant became famous throughout Europe. It was introduced into Britain by Augustine, and in A.D. 690 Benedict Biscop brought to Wearmouth John, the arch-chanter of St Peter's, Rome. All the monasteries came to learn from him, and so the Roman hours became the hours of the Anglo-Saxon Church. For their further development we must wait for the Middle Ages.

It is now possible for us to look at Christian worship in the early Church as a whole, drawing together the various threads, and seeking to discern the pattern which had been woven. Running through it all we can discern the liturgical principle, the setting forth of the saving acts of God. This is clearest in Baptism and Holy Communion. The one gathers round the Creed, and is set in the context of the Easter Vigil with its great service of Commemoration. The other, at the heart of the service in the consecration prayer as well as in its extended lections, sets before men the great things God has done for them, with the Cross, the resurrection and ascension as their consummation. In both sacraments of the Gospel this work of God for men is brought near, made operative by the work of the Holy Spirit; and by the opening of the heart to this present activity of God his gifts are received. This liturgical principle is further extended first to the Christian year but also to the week and the day. The Christian year brings before men one by one the cardinal doctrines of the Church, each centring in an act of God. Especially in the West this is emphasized by what became known as "The Proper", the special lessons, psalms, and prayers appointed for each season, and indeed for each Sunday of the year. It is thus that the full-orbed faith is kept before men. Later, the commemoration of martyrs and heroes of the faith strengthened men's hold on the historical continuity of the Church back to the time of the Apostles; strengthened, too, their grasp of the meaning of the Church itself as "the Communion of Saints". The week was similarly sanctified by the Sunday festival and the fasts of Wednesday and Friday; the day, first by private prayer and Bible-reading and later by the ordered round of worship, the offering of the Church, giving glory to God. That worship is our inheritance.

3

Worship in the Medieval Church

THE history of Christian worship in the West is the history of the expansion of the Roman rite. Originally there were two types of service in Western Europe: the Italian, represented by Rome and Milan; and the so-called Gallican, representing Spain, France, and Britain. Only slowly did the Roman type of service prevail, partly through the work of missionaries like St Augustine of Canterbury, partly through voluntary adoption; but in the end, though not uninfluenced by the rites it displaced, it became the normal use of Western Christendom. Only in southern Spain, where the Church was cut off by Moorish domination from the rest of Christendom, did the "Gallican" rite survive. England, on the other hand, after the Anglo-Saxon invasions, was a heathen country. Here the Roman rite came in with Augustine, and after a brief conflict with the Gallican rite, represented by the Northern mission of Aidan from Scottish Iona, was adopted for the whole country. It was with Roman missions that it was introduced into Germany by the Englishman Boniface, and into Scandinavia, Moravia, Bohemia, Hungary, and Poland. But the process was not one of simple displacement. Where the two rites met it was inevitable that some measure of fusion would take place, and this is exactly what we find.

The position of England was unique in the West. After Wilfred's victory at the Synod of Whitby in 664 the Anglo-Saxon Church adopted the Roman rite introduced by Augustine. Cut off from the Continent by the sea, with the Gallican rite banished, England remained far more Roman than the dominion of Charlemagne. It was only from the tenth century onwards that Gallican rites were introduced from the Continent. What we find in the Middle Ages in England is, then, a type of service which is, in the main, Roman, but with some Gallican admixture. There was no complete uniformity, for diocesan uses varied. Cranmer's preface to the Prayer Book of 1549, now headed, "Concerning the Service of the Church", mentions the Uses of Salisbury (or Sarum), Hereford, Bangor, York, and Lincoln. Of these, Sarum, York, and Hereford, in that order, were the most influential, and in southern England Sarum was much the best known, and is the basis of Cranmer's revision.

So far we have been dealing with the synthesis of Roman and Gallican rites as represented by the Sacramentary. Roughly the same is true of the daily services; but there was the additional complication of the monastic, Benedictine, Office, which differed both from the Roman and the Gallican. In England, unlike France, many of the cathedrals were served by monks, and their use differed from that of other cathedrals served by secular clergy, and of course from other churches in the same diocese. The hour services were therefore a mixture of Roman, Gallican, and Benedictine uses; but it was the Roman use which was basic—for example in the all-important use of the Psalter. A further fact of much greater importance for our understanding of the English Reformation and the making of the Prayer Book was the revision of the hour services carried out in the thirteenth century, popularized by the Franciscans and imposed on most of the churches in Europe in 1277. It was marked by the increase of Saints' days and festivals displacing the normal daily offices. The reading of Scripture was curtailed; readings from the lives of the Saints, sometimes mythical, increased; the orderly reading of the Psalter broken up by the increased observance of Festivals, and the Office of the Blessed Virgin Mary added. The new office was much shorter than the old one, but it was more complicated and has been described as "a veritable revolution in liturgy". More important, the daily services in fact became the concern of the clergy only, who could now use a portable service book.

Before we come to consider the services themselves a number of general considerations need to be discussed. First it has to be remembered that all the services of the Church, with the exception of the plighting of troth in the marriage service, were in Latin, and Latin was understood only by a small educated minority. The principle that worship should be in the tongue of the people was observed in the early Church. For at least two hundred years Greek was the *lingua franca* of the Empire, and hence even at Rome Christians spoke and wrote the Greek, which was the language of worship. Latin succeeded Greek as the common language in Western Europe and North Africa, and Latin became the liturgical language, and survived the break-up of the Empire. It cannot be denied that the use of a common language, even liturgically, has great advantages as a unifying medium, but there is little doubt that its retention was really due to a conservatism which in matters of religion is always strong. Thus the Russian Church used the old Slavonic, though it had become a dead tongue, and Coptic is used in Egypt, where Arabic is now universally spoken. It was this use of Latin in the Middle Ages which, side by side with the complexity of the services, effectually prevented congregational worship, and contributed to the separation of clergy from laity. Inevitably the clergy became the agents of the laity to perform work on their behalf rather than leaders of corporate worship.

The second important factor in the religious situation was that printing was not known until the very end of the fifteenth century— Caxton, in England, was at work *c.* 1480—and all books were necessarily manuscript, and therefore expensive. The provision of the needs even of an ordinary parish church entailed considerable expense, for before the Reformation the services of the Church were inevitably distributed through a considerable number of MSS. books.[1] The four great books, the Breviary for daily services, the Missal for the altar, the Manual for occasional offices, and the Processional for the litanies, were normally broken up for convenience into smaller books of which the greater churches would possess a number of copies. Even a small country parish was put to considerable expense in replacing them as they got worn with use. The very use of these books was, moreover, intricate and complicated. Cranmer's statement in the preface to his First Prayer Book is strictly accurate, "The number and the hardness of the Rules called the Pie, and the manifold changings of the service, was the cause, that to turn the Book only was so hard and intricate a matter, that many times there was more business to find out what should be read, than to read

[1] Cf. Swete, *Services and Service Books before the Reformation.*

it when it was found out." The position, then, was very different from that of to-day when a printed copy of the services can be put in the hand of every worshipper, and the layman can become as well acquainted with the text as the priest. The combination of Latin, intricacy, and manuscript books destroyed all possibility of an instructed, worshipping laity. The layman therefore was content to hear Mass, and, if educated, to use the Primer. The Primer was the layman's book of devotion of which several MSS. survive, those of the thirteenth century in Latin, of the fourteenth in English. Its centre was the Hours of the Virgin, dating from the eleventh century, the penitential Psalms, and the Mattins and Evensong of the Office for the Dead, in addition to the Creed, Lord's Prayer, *Ave Maria*, and the Decalogue. It was used privately and for devotion during the hearing of Mass. Thus, even for the educated, who alone could afford and use such books, the central worship of the Church, now called the Mass, was not a service shared but heard, not even followed except in spirit and intention, and with the faith that the worshipper shared in the fruits of what was effected on his behalf at the altar. Thus a liturgical revolution has taken place between the life of the early Church and that of the Middle Ages. Sooner or later, if it was to be true to the New Testament, the worship of the Body of Christ had to be restored.

We can now attempt a brief sketch of medieval worship in practice. In parish churches theoretically there was daily Mass at about nine o'clock, or noon on fast days. But almost every parish church had other altars, and town churches several chantries endowed for the saying of Masses for the souls of the departed. Guilds, too, had their altars in the parish churches, sometimes, as in Bristol, scattered through the many churches of the town, sometimes, as at Coventry, concentrated in the one great church of St Michael. There was thus abundant opportunity for hearing Mass. The worshippers would use a Primer or say the private prayers which the priest was charged to teach his people from the pulpit. That duty was, however, as episcopal visitations prove, frequently neglected. Few communicated, or to use the medieval term, were houselled more than three times a year, once a year being the minimum required. To prepare for communion men were shriven, a chair for the priest to hear confessions being placed at a side-altar when there was no permanent seat. The Sunday Mass was, however, more truly congregational, for the

28

congregation could at least share in the fixed chants, sung in parish churches to an invariant setting. It was preceded by Mattins, and the procession round the church or churchyard, originally with the singing of the Litany. Vespers, or Evensong, at two or three in the afternoon concluded Sunday observance. Preaching was rare until the fourteenth century. There are few pulpits earlier than that date, and the vast majority are a century later. Pews, too, were a very late introduction, and are roughly of the same date as pulpits. It has, however, to be remembered that at least the outline of the faith could be learned from painted glass, and in a lesser degree from the wall-painting with which medieval churches were covered. Even making full allowance for this it cannot be denied that, cut off from worship in their own tongue, with no direct knowledge of the Bible, and oftimes untaught, despite episcopal exhortation and injunction, the simple laity were wholly dependent on a priesthood who "controlled" the sacramental channels of grace. Nor did this cease with death, for the welfare of the departed was believed to be very largely dependent on the saving efficacy of propitiatory masses offered on their behalf.

The daily services, the Divine service, or in monastic churches, the Choir office, lay outside the ken of ordinary folk except, as we have seen, for Mattins and Evensong on Sundays. It had become a clerical duty only, and only in the monasteries was it fully performed. There the long night office of Mattins was said about two o'clock in the morning, followed immediately by Lauds with *Te Deum* interposed on Sundays and festivals. After a bare three hours of sleep Prime was said at six and daily Mass. Terce, Sext, and None were brief at nine o'clock, noon, and three, followed by Vespers or Evensong at five or six o'clock. Compline at seven in winter and eight in summer completed the day. The parish priest was given more liberty. All that really mattered for him was that the offices were said; in fact at the end of the Middle Ages they were normally combined and said through in two portions only. The structure of our English morning and evening prayer is, however, derived from the medieval Sarum Hours, and a brief analysis of their content is therefore given in Note 1.

The Mass, however, was all important, and significant changes had taken place since the early centuries. In the first place it had ceased to be a corporate act of the whole Church and had become, in effect, a priestly act performed on behalf of the Church. Communion had become infrequent, and the fact that the service was in Latin meant that an undue emphasis was placed on what was seen rather than on what was heard and done. Even more important, the primitive understanding of consecration as effected by thanksgiving had in the course of the centuries been displaced by the theory of consecration by the words of institution. The language used increasingly stresses the miraculous character of the change in the elements. Tertullian had used the word *figura*, "the figure of his body", and spoke of the cup as "representing Christ's blood". Cyprian, like the "Apostolic Constitutions", uses "show". Here the relationship of the Body and Blood of Christ is dynamic: they are the mystery by which the reality is manifested and by means of which it is received. But as early as Cyril of Jerusalem the language of "change" or transformation is used, and the consecrated elements become awful and fearful. Ambrose in the West similarly uses "transform", while Alcuin speaks of "consecrated" into the substance of the Body, and by the ninth century we find "change into the substance of the Body". In the final stage the consecrated elements appear to be bread and wine, since their accidents remain, but the substance, the real thing, is now the true Body and Blood of Christ; even, it was held, to flesh and bones and hair. Side by side with this emphasis on the presence of Christ in the elements went a parallel emphasis in the West on the sacrificial aspect of the Eucharist. The priest at his ordination was given the charge to offer sacrifice for the living and the dead, itself a late insertion into the Ordinal. The sacrifice of the Mass *was* in medieval thought the sacrifice of Calvary wherein the real Body and Blood of Christ were offered to the Father for the sins of men; and it availed both for the living and for souls in purgatory.

This theological development was bound to have its effect upon the service itself. The moment of consecration and the solemn oblation of the sacrifice of the Christ, present beneath the veils of the elements, became the climax of the service. Everything led up to it, and when the sacrifice was offered those present and those for whom it was intended, whether living or departed, shared in its benefits. In comparison with this—the sacrifice of the Mass—the other aspects of the service mattered little. In a sense the service ceased to be a sacrament except to the priest who communicated. The sense of the Church, of the Body of Christ realizing its unity by communion with its Head, sharing the one loaf and the one cup was bound to decline. Deeper still, the thought of God became inevitably of one who constantly required propitiation, the stern judge and not the loving Father. Even the thought of the living, victorious Christ, the conqueror of death and the giver of true life to his people was bound to be obscured by the concentration of emphasis upon atoning death. Devotion to our Lord there was, indeed. But increasingly it was devotion to his humanity, concentrated upon his suffering. The empty cross on the altar was now filled with the figure of Christ in the agony of death, and the same figure stood on the rood over the chancel: a significant change from the Christ of Glory depicted in the apses of the early basilicas. It is hardly too much to say that men had come to worship a different God and a different Christ from that of the early Church. But the difference between the early and the medieval Church had one further consequence. Because its doctrine of the Eucharist had ceased to be dynamic; because, strictly speaking, revelation was no longer necessary, the primitive balance was lost: the whole service moves from man to God, and the movement from God to man in loving self-giving virtually disappears.

The Reformers were therefore faced with a most difficult liturgical problem. They desired to restore the New Testament conception of God as the Father of our Lord Jesus Christ, making himself known to men through word and sacrament. That meant that the Mass had to become once again a communion. Their doctrine of the presence of Christ in the Sacrament must be that of the New Testament and the early Church, and this must be made clear by the service itself. And the service must once again become the service of the Church, the Body of Christ, which meant not only more frequent communion but corporate, congregational, worship. And yet they were conservative. They were English Churchmen: they shared the heritage of Western Christendom. Their work had therefore to be done within the framework of the existing service. That problem is almost insoluble without a more radical departure from the past than Englishmen then or now are prepared to allow. But the attempt was made, and to it we must in due course come.

So far we have dealt only with the sacraments of the Gospel (for the primitive pattern of the Baptismal Office remained unchanged) and with the daily service. There remain the Litany and the Occasional Offices which must be much more briefly treated.

The Litany we have already mentioned as part of the Holy Communion service of the early Church. The first part of the Prayers of the Faithful when the catechumens and penitents had left was the deacon's Litany, to each prayer of which the people replied, *Kyrie eleison*, Lord have mercy. This diaconal Litany has always remained a part of the Eastern service. There was nothing exactly corresponding to it in the West, though at a later period a Litany was introduced, now represented by the nine-fold Kyrie, and in our English service by the response to the commandments. The Litany was also used at the beginning of the Mass in the ordination service (where it still stands), after the Blessing of the font on Easter eve, at the consecration of churches, and after Terce in Lent.

Beside the "stational" Litany, said or sung kneeling, there were processional Litanies first introduced by St John Chrysostom as a counter-attraction to the processions of the Arians. Such processions with responsorial singing were penitential in tone, but soon became popular, and were introduced into the West in 467 when the last volcanic eruptions of the Auvergnes, with accompanying earthquakes, devastated the church of Vienne in Gaul. The bishop, Mamertus, ordered penitential processions beseeching God's mercy on the Monday, Tuesday, and Wednesday before Ascension. Thus the Rogationtide Litany began, spread through Gaul, and in the ninth century was adopted at Rome. At Rome itself we find in the time of Gregory the Great, *c.* 598, the custom of a processional litany from the Church of St Lawrence, on St Mark's Day, 25 April, which is the date of the ancient pagan festival, the Robigalia. The custom of observing St Mark's Day became universal, and its litany known as Litania maior—the great litany. Bede tells us that Augustine and his monks came to Canterbury in 597 singing a Litany. The observance of the Rogationtide and St Mark's-tide processions was made obligatory in England by the Council of Clovesho in 747 and processions on penitential occasions became popular in Anglo-Saxon England where they were known as gang-days. Their popularity remained, and medieval England was famous for the devotion of its processions. Every church possessed its Processional or book of Litanies: and of these the Sarum Litany, or Litany of the Saints, became the basis of our English Litany in 1544, the first source to be translated into the mother tongue. The Sunday Litany before Mass, originally a processional Litany round the church, survived only in the form of a mere procession.

Of the two services which concern the crises of men's lives, marriage and burial, the former need not concern us except to notice that its setting is, as we should expect, the Mass. The marriage service, derived from the pre-Christian Roman rites, survives almost unchanged in our English Prayer Book. Part of it was already in English before the Reformation. But the burial service has been radically altered, and some account of the medieval rites must therefore be given.

Christianity brought into the world a new conception of death—"to be with Christ", and a new hope—"the resurrection of the body". Death was both rest and victory: the early Christian could write of his dead: *Requiescit in pace*—"He rests in peace". Of the early services we know little more than that it was a carrying to the tomb with Psalms and hymns and probably lights. We know, too, that the departed were commemorated at the Eucharist with the sense of fellowship with them in Christ. But prayer soon became less certain in tone. From being prayer for light and blessing it is now made directly for the soul of the dead, for delivery from the consequences of sin, and such prayers are included in the Sacramentaries. The Penitential of Archbishop Theodore (Archbishop of Canterbury in 666) says: "Following the Roman Church, the custom is for monks or religious men to carry the dead into the church, and to anoint their breasts with chrism and there to celebrate masses on their behalf: then, with singing, to carry them to burial and having placed them in the tomb, to pour out prayer for them." The essentials of the medieval rite are already present.

The Sarum rite sped the departing with prayers and a solemn farewell in the name of the Trinity. The soul was commended to God, and the penitential Psalms were sung while the body was prepared for burial and carried to church. There the Evensong (*Placebo*) and the Mattins with Lauds (*Dirige*) were said while the body lay before the altar. Requiem Mass, so called from its introit (*Requiem aeternam dona eis Domine, et lux perpetua luceat eis*), was sung, and the body was censed and sprinkled with holy water. The Absolutions of the Dead were read, and Psalms were sung while the grave, already marked with the cross and sprinkled with holy water, was dug. The body was placed in the grave, earth placed on it in the form of the cross, a final collect for forgiveness was said—sometimes a written absolution was placed on the breast—and the returning procession sang the penitential Psalms.

After burial the Office of the Dead was repeated during the following month and thirty masses, a trental, said for the departed. There is little doubt that this rite, with its consistently sombre tone, represents a real departure from the tradition of the early Church. In the Greek Orthodox Church the burial service is not part of the Liturgy; and the note of sin and punishment is far less marked in the prayers than in the West, where it is dominant. The doctrine of the West concerning the future life was dominated by the thought of purgatory, beginning with the speculations of Augustine and made dogma, with terrifying disclosures of its horrors, by Gregory the Great. That was why the Office of the Dead was included in the Primers, why men were so consistently exhorted to contemplate death and its consequences, and why, at the very close of the Middle Ages, the sale of indulgences for the souls of the departed could become so lucrative a trade. It was also why the English Reformers abandoned the whole conception of purgatory and removed prayers for the departed from the services of the Church.

4

Worship and the Reformation

THE Reformation in England in its vital phase, when the English Prayer Books were produced, came comparatively late; practically a generation after Luther's break with Rome. No important doctrinal or liturgical changes were possible during the lifetime of Henry the Eighth, but this meant that Cranmer had time to prepare his work carefully. He was a good scholar, his private library was larger than that of his own University of Cambridge, and slowly but surely he had arrived at his own doctrinal position. Moreover, when Henry died, Cranmer had been Archbishop of Canterbury for nearly fourteen years, and already had succeeded, for the credit is chiefly his, in setting up the English Bible in every church in the land. The Injunctions of 1538 required the clergy "expressly to provoke, stir, and exhort every person to read the same", and every incumbent was to recite the Paternoster, Creed, and Ten Commandments in English that his flock might learn them by degrees. Cranmer's mind had begun to move away from the old learning of the Middle Ages even before Luther's work as a Reformer began, but his serious New Testament study began with the publication of Erasmus's New Testament in 1516, and so virtually coincided with the publication of Luther's ninety-five theses. It has, however, to be remembered that the memory of Wycliffe was not dead in England, and that his works were known and read. Heresy was already being punished by the stake under Archbishop Warham, and More owned in 1516 that attacks on the clergy were popular. It is a mistake to suppose that the Reformation in England is simply the pale reflection of the Continental Lutheranism and Calvinism. It was, of course, affected by them, but it was, at least partly, an independent movement, and it remained essentially English. That this was so is in great measure due to Cranmer.

Cranmer's character was vilified by his enemies, but Pollard's estimate[1] is just: "In him was no guile; his variations were not calculated, but the faithful reflex of developing convictions. He was never a victim of that infirmity which leads men to pretend that they have always held the same inflexible principles." His convictions changed as men's must in days of creative transition, but he spared no pains to arrive at them. He was one of the most learned men of his age. He read his Bible from cover to cover, himself translating the Old Testament from Hebrew to Latin. He possessed an almost complete set of the Greek and Latin Fathers, and was familiar with them. He read the Continental Reformers and made careful excerpts from their writings and besides Latin, Greek, and Hebrew, read French, Italian, and German. We know that his liturgical studies were wide; indeed by the standards of his day he was probably the greatest liturgical scholar not only in England but in Europe, and no Englishman in the next two hundred years possessed his knowledge. This, however, does not mean that he possessed the knowledge which we have today. He highly regarded the early Fathers, "who were nearest unto Christ's time, and therefore might best know the truth", but he had no liturgical documents earlier than the developed liturgies of the East and West. Documents such as the *Didaché*, the *Apostolic Tradition* of Hippolytus, the *Sacramentary* of Sarapion had not been discovered in his day, whereas for us they are of first importance. Nor could he know, as we do now, the Jewish background of early Christian worship; and, in particular, that the true basis for the understanding of the great Eucharistic prayer—what we call the consecration prayer—is the Jewish thanksgiving or blessing of God, said over food and drink in a fellowship meal. He had to use the data at his disposal: the medieval services, the writings of the Fathers and the New Testament; and, despite his deep desire to return to scriptural truth and primitive practice, the influence of the late medieval practice of his day remained, whether in reaction from it, or in unconscious acceptance of it. His work, moreover, had to be carried out in a situation always difficult, and often dangerous. He was a reformer,

[1] A. F. Pollard, *Thomas Cranmer*, p. 317.

and the sheer weight of religious conservatism was against him. His colleagues were men of incomparably less learning, and with far less balance and judgment. The political background, especially in the latter part of Edward the Sixth's reign, is one of the really disgraceful periods of English history. But his work endured, and to it we must come.

During Henry the Eighth's reign little could be done; for the King, though he broke with the Papacy, had no sympathy with the Reformation. Cranmer had, however, come to see that there could be no real reform in worship until the services were in the common tongue. Largely through his efforts the English Bible was set up in every parish church in 1538 that it might be read out of service time, but no exposition was allowed. In 1543 a chapter of the New Testament was ordered to be read in English after *Te Deum* at Mattins and after *Magnificat* at Evensong. It is at least partly true that it was the translation of the Bible, Tyndale's incomparable work, which was the cause of the English Prayer Book. Then, in 1544, the Litany was ordered to be said in English, for Henry was at war with both France and Scotland, and the response to the usual processions had been poor. This was attributed to the use of Latin, and the King ordered Cranmer to produce an English form. The fact that the long series of invocation of saints, which had given to the Sarum service its common title "The Litany of the Saints", was reduced to three clauses, is evidence of the movement towards reform.

Edward the Sixth came to the throne in January, 1547, and at the close of the year the cup was restored to the laity. A short English form (consisting of an Exhortation, a form of confession and absolution, the Comfortable Words, the Prayer of Humble Access, the words of administration, and the benediction) was therefore produced in 1548, and was inserted into the Latin Mass immediately after the priest's communion. The first step has been taken towards the transformation of the Mass into a Communion. It was, however, only a first step, and the Preface foreshadowed further changes. By the end of the year a task had been completed which marks the great turning point in the history of English worship; the first English Prayer Book was ready, and came into use on Whitsunday, 1549. It contained no Ordinal, which in the Middle Ages had been the bishop's book, and no printed Psalter, but only a Table showing how the Psalms were to

37

be read in a monthly course; otherwise it covered all the services of the Church. Its publication was a revolutionary step. The whole was in English, the superb English of Cranmer, never surpassed except perhaps by Tyndale's. One book took the place of many, a book which all could read, and the price of which, bound, was limited to "three shillings and eight pence the piece". The result had not been achieved without the sacrifice of many things beautiful in themselves; the product of centuries of careful elaboration. Even the lovely hymns of the hour services disappeared, for Cranmer was no poet. But the cost had been counted, and the sacrifice was worth while. This first Prayer Book is, as Cranmer himself insisted, a work of the Reformation, yet it was a conservative reform. It contained material taken from Continental sources, but the heart of the book is still Sarum. It is an English Prayer Book, not only in its language but in its sane conservatism.

In November of the same year all the old service books were ordered to be destroyed except Henry the Eighth's Primer, and even there the invocation of saints was to be blotted out. All images in churches were to be destroyed. It was a drastic step, but Cranmer had been impressed with the realization that the Latin image was the equivalent of the Greek *eidōlon* from which our English idol is derived, and images had to go. We may regret the loss of much beautiful work, and much of the destruction now seems to us sheer vandalism, but from the standpoint of the Reformers the doctrinal issue was all-important: the saints as mediators had become between man and God, and the superstition must be destroyed, however great the cost.

In 1550 the reformed Ordinal was published. It was a simplification of Sarum, and produced order out of a muddled rite which was a fusion, almost a duplication, of the Roman and Gallican services. It was shorn of much of its ceremonial and its reformed emphasis is marked by the gift to the priest not only of the chalice and paten but of the Bible as the symbols of ministry, the ministry of the word and sacraments. The minor orders, doorkeeper, lector, acolyte, and sub-deacon were abolished, but the historic three-fold ministry of bishop, presbyter and deacon was retained.

This completes the first phase of the Reformation in Edward the Sixth's reign. The first Prayer Book was a compromise. Mainly the work of Cranmer, it had been modified by Parliament, and did not satisfy the more extreme Reformers. Its Eucharistic doctrine is neither Lutheran nor Calvinist; it was liturgically a book which Cranmer alone could have produced, incorporating as it did elements of Eastern as well as Western use. Cranmer, indeed, was not a theologian in the sense that Luther or Calvin was. His abiding greatness is liturgical rather than theological. He came to accept the fundamental dogmas of the Reformation, the supremacy of Scripture, justification by faith and unmediated access of every soul to God; but his approach, like that of most Englishmen, was essentially practical. He wanted to reform abuses and to do it, as far as possible, acceptably. His own note at the end of the Book: "Of ceremonies, why some be abolished and some retained", expresses his own mind. Ceremonies which serve a godly and decent order are to be retained. "For in such case they ought rather to have reverence unto them for their antiquity, if they will declare themselves to be more studious of unity and concord, than of innovations and new-fangledness, which (as much as may be with true setting forth of Christ's religion) is always to be eschewed." The one criterion by which he was prepared to judge and to act was Holy Scripture, of which he was a lifelong student. It was this study, together with his consciousness of current abuses, and not his wide knowledge of the writings of Continental reformers, which conditioned his liturgical reforms.

The first Prayer Book satisfied nobody. On the one hand, religious conservatism made its novelties unacceptable; on the other, men like Ridley, Hooper, and John Knox wanted a much more thoroughgoing reform. Moreover, in 1549 Somerset had fallen and the regime of Northumberland which followed was one of sheer oppression in the interest of rich landlords. "Never", it has been said, "did Henry the Eighth, or Charles the First, or James the Second, aim such blows at English liberties as the men who controlled the fate of the Reformation in the latter days of Edward the Sixth.' This was sheer tragedy, for the Reformation in England was winning its way, especially in the towns; and men like Knox and Hooper made Cranmer's work far more difficult by their adulation of Northumberland as "a most holy and fearless instrument of the Word of God".

The reforming party was further strengthened by a group of foreign Reformers brought to England by Cranmer as the nucleus of a Protestant Council. Bucer, who stood, theologically, between

Luther and Calvin, had been made Regius Professor of Divinity at Cambridge; Peter Martyr, who knew the Swiss Reformers, came to Oxford; John A'Lasco, a follower of Calvin, was in London superintending the German and Dutch Protestant congregation. Bucer in 1551 sent to Cranmer his *Censura*, a critical examination of the first Prayer Book. This work was undoubtedly influential, but not so influential as the views of Hooper and Coverdale, and those who, like them, had fled to the Continent in Henry's reign, and returned under Edward determined to propagate the doctrines they had imbibed. Cranmer himself had been forced into controversy by Gardiner, who sought to show that the doctrine of the real presence of Christ in the elements could be held consistently with the use of the 1549 Prayer Book; a view which the Archbishop repudiated in his *Defence of the True and Catholic Doctrine of the Sacrament* of 1550 and *An Answer* of 1551, in which he deals both with Gardiner's attack and that of Dr Richard Smith published in Louvain. It was this refusal from the Catholic side to accept the first Prayer Book as a truly Reformed work, and the determined attempt to interpret its language as consonant with the pre-Reformation doctrines, which convinced Cranmer that a new book was required, and that this time its language must be beyond all cavil.

By the end of 1551 the new book was ready, and its use from All Saints' Day, 1552, was legalized by the Second Act of Uniformity which prescribes attendance at church by the laity and imprisonment for attendance elsewhere. Every passage cited by Gardiner as giving colour to the old belief was altered or expunged. The Consecration Prayer was broken up by the insertion of the Communion at its heart, immediately after the words of Institution; and both the Prayer of Oblation and the Prayer of Humble Access were so placed that their language could not be construed as referring to the elements. The *Benedictus* and *Agnus Dei* were omitted; the terms mass and altar disappeared, as did also invocation of the saints and prayers for the dead. The words of administration of the Sacrament were significantly changed so that the elements were not called the Body and Blood of Christ. The Mass vestments, allowed with a cope as the alternative in the first Prayer Book, were swept away. Similar changes were made in the occasional offices. Anointing, exorcism, and the white chrysom robe disappeared from Holy Baptism, the sign of the cross remaining only here in the Prayer Book; the celebration of Holy Communion at funerals was no longer contemplated, though it was retained at the marriage service. The need for private confession was still further lessened by the provision of a form of confession and absolution as a penitential introduction to morning and evening prayer.

As Edward the Sixth died in July, 1553, this second Prayer Book was only in use for eight months before Mary swept away the work of her brother's reign and by her policy of persecution established what he sought to destroy. On Elizabeth's accession, five years later, it was the Prayer Book of 1552 which was restored with only two significant changes: the omission of the "Black Rubric"[1]; and the combination of the 1549 and 1552 words of administration of the sacrament. The further additions and modifications of 1604 and 1662 left its character essentially unchanged. This does not, of course, mean that the Anglican Divines of the late sixteenth and seventeenth centuries all shared Cranmer's "second thoughts"; the Communion service of the Scottish Prayer Book is clear evidence to the contrary. But the 1662 Book is basically that of 1552 not that of 1549; only in 1928 was the abortive attempt made to authorize what was substantially 1549 as an alternative. The attempts of the Puritans to carry liturgical reform still further both in Elizabeth's reign and in the seventeenth century ended, as indeed they were bound to end, only in schism: but they left the Anglican Church spiritually impoverished, and with an enfeebled understanding of the worship which her Liturgy enshrined. Even to-day what is most needed is a clearer understanding of the theological implications of Cranmer's work.

In undertaking this task we are not left wholly dependent upon the Prayer Book itself. The supreme field of Cranmer's genius was, as we have seen, liturgical, but he was a trained theologian, though not a creative thinker: and as a theologian he knew that in the final analysis worship is dependent upon doctrine. As early as 1549 he drew up Articles which preachers and lecturers subscribed as a condition of obtaining his licence; and in 1551 submitted them, or a similar list, to the Episcopate. In May, 1552, the Council demanded their production, and the authority by which they had been set forth, and then appointed a committee of six divines, including Knox, to

[1] For Black rubric see Note 3.

revise them. Their amendments were submitted to the Archbishop and were set forth by royal authority and probably without the consent of Convocation, despite the assertion of their title page. The exact measure of authority to be ascribed to these Articles is for our purposes unimportant. The important facts are that they are contemporary with the second Prayer Book, are mainly the work of Cranmer, and that substantially they form the basis of our present, fully-authoritative Thirty-nine Articles. Clearly they are aimed at Rome on the one hand and Anabaptism on the other, but in the frequently quoted phrase of Dixon: "The broad, soft touch of Cranmer lay upon them." The controversies between the different schools of thought of the Reformation are characteristically avoided, for Cranmer's whole attitude towards them was eirenical. But that does not mean that his own position was not essentially reformed. Like all the English Reformers he accepted the doctrine of justication by faith only—*justificatio ex sola fide Jesu Christi*—in the words of the Article[1]; he rejected the whole conception of infused grace, or that the Sacraments contain grace; denied that sacraments are effective *ex opere operato*, and explicitly rejected the doctrine of the real presence of Christ in the elements of the Lord's Supper. Not only so, but the conception of the Mass as a propitiatory sacrifice was expressly repudiated in the Article "Of the Perfect Oblation of Christ made upon the Cross", and at length by Cranmer in the fifth book of his *Defence of the True and Catholic Doctrine Concerning the Sacrament.* The doctrine of purgatory had already been abandoned by Cranmer as early as 1537 and our present Article 22 closely follows that of 1553.

Now if we ask on what ground these doctrines are accepted or rejected the answer is at once clear alike from Article 5 of 1553 and from Cranmer's works. The appeal is to Holy Scripture, and secondarily, but in quite a different sense, to the Fathers and the practice of the early Church. The Anglican Reformers believed that they were restoring the worship of the Church to its primitive purity and simplicity, but doctrinally, on the supremacy of Scripture and the doctrine of justification by faith, their whole work stands or falls. It is, however, possible to deduce from this doctrinal setting the

[1] The article refers to the Homily on Justification, where the doctrine is fully treated: and this homily was Cranmer's own work, though probably derived from Melancthon's Commonplaces.

principles of worship on which implicitly the Prayer Book is built. First the doctrine of the priesthood of all believers and the rejection of a sacerdotal or mediatorial conception of the ministry means that worship must be corporate, the worship of the Church, and must therefore be in the common tongue. Not only so, but it must be understood by those who share in it. This, to Cranmer, meant that it must be simple. "Dark or dumb ceremonies" must be abolished; the Calendar must be simplified: anthems, responds, however beautiful, must be omitted if they prevent simple folk from following the service; exhortations must be introduced to make clear what is being done, the perfect example being the opening exhortation of morning and evening prayer. And what was done on a small scale within any particular service was done on the grand scale as well. The hour services were reduced to two, and of similar form, the reading of the Psalter arranged for a straightforward monthly course. But secondly worship must not only be simple but scriptural, and this means much more than the orderly reading of the Bible. This, indeed, Cranmer provided by the simplest of expedients, the reading of a chapter of the Old and New Testaments daily at Mattins and Evensong, and in so doing he effected a profound transformation of the daily offices. "Thy Word is a lantern unto my feet", said E. C. Ratcliff, might be their motto. But Cranmer's deeper principle is expressed by the verse of Romans 10: "Faith cometh by hearing, and hearing by the Word of God." Worship for the Reformers was essentially the response of faith to the word of God. Bible reading, sermons, sacraments were various modes of that one word, and this is the determining factor in all Cranmer's work. The Bible is given to the priest and bishop alike at ordination as the symbol of their work, the sermon is restored to Holy Communion, there is a wholly new emphasis on preaching, and the Comfortable words are introduced to add the assurance of Holy Scripture to the Church's absolution. But the same truth is applied to the service of Holy Communion —the mediation of the word by means of sacrament. Here, too, the essential movement of the service is transformed. The heart of it now is reception by faith: the response is that spiritual worship which alone is acceptable to God, the oblation, the living sacrifice of soul and body. The most difficult of all Cranmer's liturgical problems was how to effect this in his service. He did it eventually, in the second

Prayer Book, by inserting Communion into the consecration prayer itself, directly following the Words of Institution and before the Lord's Prayer. His action to this day has been bitterly criticized by liturgiologists whose criteria are the ancient and medieval liturgies, but the principle at stake was fundamental. The doctrine of the sacrifice of the Mass with the parallel doctrine of a sacrificing priesthood was clean contrary to the doctrine of justification as the Reformers understood it. It made Communion of quite secondary importance; it obscured the truth that man's response of faith is elicited by God's self-giving of which the Cross is the all-sufficient ground and assurance. For the Reformers the status of Christian men as sons of God is secure in Christ, despite their sinfulness, and in Christ they have direct access to the Father. Propitiatory sacrifice offered on their behalf by a priest was therefore dishonouring to God.[1] Everything therefore which could be construed as implying a sacrificial rite was removed, the terms Mass and altar, distinctive vestments, stone altars, the eastward position of the celebrant, the oblation of the elements. By contrast the Communion aspect was emphasized. The table was to be of wood and movable, so that it could be brought down the chancel step. It was covered with a fair linen cloth and the minister was to stand so that his actions could be seen; for the rite was to be understood as the service of the Upper Room and the worshippers were to understand it as the proclamation of Christ's death: not a memorial before God but an *anamnesis*, a bringing to remembrance before men. Finally, non-communicating attendance was forbidden; the service was to be Communion or it was nothing. What the Reformers sought to do was not only to destroy the Mass but to restore the Communion. Their ideal was that of the primitive and early Church, a ministry of word and sacrament intimately conjoined Sunday by Sunday; a Communion of the Body and Blood of Christ shared by all, and side by side with it a daily office in which the scriptures read and the Psalms said or sung in unbroken course should build men up in the faith. We have now to see how and how far that ideal was achieved.

[1] Cf. Cranmer, *The Lord's Supper*, Parker Soc., p. 345. "The greatest blasphemy and injury that can be against Christ, and yet universally used throughout the Popish kingdom, is this, that the priests make their Mass a sacrifice propitiatory, to remit the sins as well of themselves as of others, both quick and dead, to whom they list to apply the same."

5

The Making of the Prayer Book 1549—1662

THE first official step for the Reform of the Breviary, that is of the daily services, was taken in Spain, where, at the request of Pope Clement VII, Cardinal Quiñonez, or Quignon, as he is usually called, produced a revised service book in 1535. Its chief aim was the restoration of consecutive reading of the Bible and the Psalter. The traditional hours of prayer were retained, but the Psalms were evenly distributed through the week, three lessons from the Old and New Testament read at Mattins, the *Te Deum* used daily, except in Advent and Lent, instead of on Sundays and Festivals only, and the Apostles' Creed substituted on week-days for the Athanasian. Quignon's title page bore the text "Search the Scriptures", and its Preface was used by Cranmer in his own Preface to the first Prayer Book. We know, in fact, that between 1543 and 1547 Cranmer drew up two schemes for the revision of the daily offices. The first is a revision of Sarum with the help of Quignon, the second is virtually a first draft of the later Prayer Book services in which Prime and Compline and the little hours are omitted.

In Germany reformation had gone much further. Luther, in 1523, produced a reformed baptismal service and Latin communion service which followed fairly closely the traditional form. The daily services remained unchanged, but the lessons were in German. In 1526 both Mass and daily services appeared in German with much greater departures from the unreformed rites. These were followed in 1529 by the Litany, which, like Cranmer's later work, omitted Invocation of the saints and added a considerable proportion of new petitions. "Solemnization of Matrimony" appeared in 1534 and "The forms of Ordination of Ministers of the Word" in 1537. In addition the two Catechisms of 1529 are important, since they provided the model for similar manuals of instruction both here and in Switzerland. Luther's rites formed a general basis for all the Protestant States of Germany, and were embodied in what are known as Church Orders. Strassburg, however, stood somewhat apart and under Bucer went further than Luther in departing from the medieval structure of the services. Calvin at Geneva and Zwingli at Zürich went further still. The most important development from the standpoint of English liturgical reform followed the Diet of Regensburg in 1541 which required the ecclesiastical authorities in Catholic Germany to reform their dioceses. Archbishop Hermann of Cologne took the revolutionary step of inviting Bucer from Strassburg and Philip Melancthon from Wittenberg to carry through the reform. This was, of course, going beyond anything which the Diet intended, and the opposition of the Cathedral Chapter led to Hermann's excommunication in 1546 and deprivation in the following year. Meanwhile, in 1542, the work of Bucer and Melanchthon, largely based on the Church Order of Osiander, was published in German, and later, in a revised form, in Latin. It is usually quoted as the *Deliberatio* or "Consultation". The greater part of it is doctrinal, but it contains more or less complete forms for Baptism, Confirmation, The Lord's Supper, Visitation and Communion of the Sick, Marriage, and Burial, the services being characterized by long, and somewhat tedious, exhortations. This document is of great importance to us because Cranmer made considerable use of it in the construction of the English occasional offices: Baptism is a good example.

It would, however, be a mistake to suppose that Cranmer's work was simply the making use of material already to hand in work done on the Continent. He was, indeed, well acquainted with what had already been attempted, but he worked independently, and with a wealth of knowledge which few, if any, of his contemporaries possessed. Moreover, he worked on a different principle. The Continental Reformation was doctrinal, through and through. Behind it lay Luther's personal conversion, as radical a change as that of St Paul or St Augustine. Cranmer seems to have passed through no such crisis. The gradual change in his convictions was, as we have seen, conditioned by the current abuses on the one hand and by the study of the New Testament in its original language on the other. By temperament he was cautious and conservative, with the result that the Reformation in England was far less radical than that of Continental countries. In England only was the threefold order of ministry retained, not indeed as a sacerdotal ministry, but as primitive. Nowhere else did the Reformation produce an Ordinal comparable with the English services, themselves a vast improvement on the medieval models. Nowhere else has a daily office survived, and even Lutheranism, with a "higher" doctrine of the Eucharist than that of the English reformers, has, until recent years, abandoned its liturgical expression. These results cannot wholly be attributed to the excellence of Cranmer's work. The English heritage of liturgical worship might have been lost but for the firmness of Elizabeth's hand in the next generation. But had it been lost, it would have been through the influence of men who throughout Mary's reign lived in Strassburg, Geneva, or Zürich. There they met with the Reformation precisely in that phase of it in which is breathed a different spirit from that of Cranmer. This distinction can be put into words quite simply. Cranmer sought to preserve the old liturgical structure of the services, simplifying it in order that worship might be truly corporate, but changing it only when it implied false doctrine, and therefore most radically in the Mass. The Continent produced, especially under Calvin's influence, a new doctrinal structure and sought to give it expression in worship. Thus within a very few years the liturgical structure of the worship progressively disappeared under the influence of the principle of conformity to Holy Scripture. The requirements of the English Puritans at the Savoy Conference of 1661 well illustrate the difference in principle between the Continental and Prayer Book systems of worship. They asked that alternation between minister and people should be omitted, "the *Holy Scriptures* intimating the people's part in public prayer to be only silence and reverence to attend thereunto, and to declare their consent in the close by saying *Amen*": that the Litany should be turned into one long prayer; that extempore prayer should not be excluded from any part of public worship; that part of the liturgy might be omitted at the discretion of the minister; that Collects should be abolished in favour of longer prayers. Even the simplest ceremonial was to be abandoned, the use of the surplice, of the Cross in Baptism and the custom of kneeling to receive Communion. Baxter did indeed produce "the Savoy Liturgy", a compromise between the Prayer Book and the Genevan rite, but the real desire of the Puritan party was for a service built round the sermon, the reading of Scripture, the Psalms, and extempore prayer, and led by one "Order" of ministry.

The Prayer Book, then, is neither Lutheran nor Calvinist (though if a comparison is to be made it lies closer to the earlier forms of Lutheranism), and this has had important consequences. What is now known as Anglicanism has grown up round, and been formed by, Prayer Book worship. That, precisely, is what is never understood on the Continent and constantly criticized as neither truly Catholic nor truly Reformed. That is also the reason why the Prayer Book and the Articles do not precisely fit. The articles were revised in Elizabeth's reign when Calvinist influence was stronger and so are Calvinist rather than Lutheran in their theology. The Anglican Evangelical has always held that the Prayer Book must be interpreted by the Articles as the doctrinal standard of the English Reformation, and logically this is correct. But nothing can alter the historical fact that they represent a slightly different phase of the English Reformation.

We must now examine Cranmer's work. The title page of the First Prayer Book to which our present book substantially conforms, reads *The Book of Common Prayer and Administration of the Sacraments, and other Rites and Ceremonies of the Church; after the use of the Church of England*. That states the fundamental position. The rites and ceremonies are those of the Church. Common Prayer is the representative of the Breviary and the Hour Services; the administration of the sacraments goes back to the Sacramentary and its medieval derivatives, the other rites and ceremonies represent the Manual. All have been reformed with a resultant English use, but the worship is the worship of the Church. Temporarily this was obscured by the second Prayer Book which spoke of "the rites and ceremonies in the Church of England", but the original emphasis was of set purpose restored in 1662.

The Preface to Cranmer's Prayer Books has now been relegated, by the much less interesting Preface of 1662, to second place where it now appears with the title "Concerning the Service of the Church". Derived from Quignon's Preface to his revised Breviary it strictly applies only to the "Divine Service", that is the daily hour services. Set, however, as a preface to the whole book, its principles govern more than Morning and Evening prayer. Corruption has taken place, and reform is needed not only in the Divine Service but in other things as well, but may be illustrated from the daily services. That corruption has come, says Cranmer, partly by the breaking-up of the orderly course of reading the Bible and Psalms; partly by its elaboration by the introduction of "responds, verses, vain repetitions"; partly by the substitution of "uncertain stories", legendary lives of the saints, for Holy Scripture. Further the Pauline principle that worship must edify so that men are built up in the faith has been nullified by the use of Latin; and, even apart from this, medieval complications make reform urgent. Cranmer therefore sets out a plain Calendar with easy rules, a form of prayer "agreeable to the mind and purpose of the Old Fathers", in which superstition has been eliminated, short and plain. Moreover, the production of one book means not only great saving of expense but the unification of diocesan uses; "now from henceforth the whole realm shall have but one use". There, briefly, are Cranmer's principles, not the production of a wholly new order but the restoration of scriptural and primitive simplicity.

At the end of the Prayer Book of 1549 there is a note, transferred in 1552 to its present place, "Of ceremonies, why some be abolished and some retained." Here, too, we can obtain light on Cranmer's outlook and insight. He recognizes the value of ceremonial for discipline and order, and at the same time the danger of excess. Even ceremonies "of godly intent and purpose" turned to vanity and superstition. Others were not only unprofitable but "blinded the people and obscured the glory of God". Others deserve to be maintained—and here the principle is stated—"because they pertain to edification; where unto all things done in the Church (as the apostle teacheth) ought to be referred". He protests that the excessive ceremonial of the medieval Church, much of it obscure in meaning, "did more confound and darken than declare and set forth Christ's benefits to us". So his canon is that a ceremony must have a direct and obvious meaning to stir up the dull mind of man. But the "most weighty cause" of abolishment was the superstition which went with ignorance, and the avarice which exploited it. Cranmer therefore was ruthless, reducing ceremonial considerably in his first Prayer Book and to a bare minimum in the second. He himself was certainly more willing than some of his colleagues to reverence antiquity, but his overriding consideration was the building up of the worshipping congregation within the framework of a decent order understood by all.

Appended to this extended note, and in small type, are a series of notes which disappeared with the second Prayer Book and have never been re-inserted, but are of interest as illustrating the liberty within a framework of order which was Cranmer's ideal. The first two deal with the vestments of the clergy. A surplice is prescribed for Mattins and Evensong, baptising and burying, and "it is seemly" that graduates wear their university hoods when they preach. "In all other places, every minister shall be at liberty to use any surplice or no."[1] The same kind of freedom belongs to the layman. "As touching, kneeling, crossing, holding up of hands, knocking upon the breast, and other gestures, they may be used or left, as every man's devotion serveth, without blame." The way in which these principles were actually applied to rites (that is services) and ceremonies must now be examined, though the details must remain for subsequent consideration.

The preface had announced a new Calendar. Beside the great Christian festivals it contained no commemorations except those of New Testament saints and All Saints. This alone was a revolutionary change, for it abolished what had been the major cause of medieval complications, namely, the number of saints' days. The Psalms followed, except for minor refinements, the now familiar, but then entirely novel, monthly cycle. There was no printed Psalter in the Prayer Book itself till 1662, so presumably the Bible was used and the Psalms read by the minister. The lessons, except those for a very few festivals and for Advent when, following ancient custom, Isaiah was read, followed not the ecclesiastical but the civil year. A

[1] The rubric before the Communion service, however, prescribes a white alb plain with vestment or cope for the celebrant and albs with tunicles for his assistants.

chapter of the Old Testament was read morning and evening till the Book was finished, and the next was then begun. At Mattins a chapter of the Gospels or Acts was read in direct sequence, and at Evensong the second lesson was always from an Epistle. Thus in January, Genesis, St Matthew and Romans were begun and read right through. Very few passages were omitted, the result being that the Old Testament was read through once in the year and the New Testament except the Book of Revelation, three times. The only significant departure from this scheme till the nineteenth century was the appointment in Elizabeth's reign of special lessons for Sundays. This change marks the recognition that, in fact, the week-day services were not attended by the laity and that Morning and Evening Prayer on Sundays require special treatment. All subsequent revisions of the lectionary and the use of the Psalter have been based implicitly on the same assumption. At the cost, then, of abandoning the Christian year, and it was no light one, Cranmer achieved the simplicity at which he aimed, and ensured the Bible should be read and known. He had, in fact, given to Holy Scripture a place in worship greater than the ancient offices had at any time provided. At the same time he reduced the daily offices to two, Mattins and Evensong[1] in 1549, Morning and Evening Prayer in 1552. Mattins was derived from Mattins and Lauds, with the Creed and third Collect from Prime; Evensong from Vespers and Compline; the little hours being wholly omitted. Both daily services were constructed on the same very simple model and their congregational character is shown by the saying of both Lord's Prayer and Creed aloud instead of privately. Cranmer, it would seem, had the laity rather than the clergy in mind in all this reconstruction. The daily services in his intention were no longer to be the exclusive concern of the clergy.

Far less radical was Cranmer's treatment of the Mass. He himself, by the autumn of 1548, had ceased to believe in the doctrine of the Real Presence, which as distinct from transubstantiation he had held for the previous decade. In the debate on the Prayer Book he said: "Our faith is not to believe Him (our Lord) to be in bread and wine, but that He is in heaven; this is proved by Scripture and Doctors." "I believe that Christ is eaten with the heart. The eating with the

[1] The old names still appear in the Table of Proper Lessons and Proper Psalms.

mouth cannot give us life, for then should a sinner have life. Only good men can eat Christ's body; and when the evil eateth the sacrament, bread and wine, he neither hath Christ's body nor eateth it." The Prayer Book was, in fact, a compromise, and though Cranmer asserted against Gardiner its essentially reformed character his own draft had, in fact, been modified by his colleagues. It closely follows the Sarum rite in English translation, but the elevation and adoration of the sacrament were omitted, the word oblation was studiously avoided and at the end of the Canon the priest says "Christ our Paschal lamb is offered up for us, once for all, when he bore our sins on his own Body upon the cross; for he is the very lamb of God, that taketh away the sins of the world; wherefore let us keep a joyful and holy feast with the Lord." Clearly the intention is to repudiate the doctrine of Eucharistic sacrifice. That the doctrine of the Real Presence is equally excluded is by no means clear, as may be seen from the rubric. "And every one (bread) shall be divided in two pieces, at the least . . . and so distributed. And men must not think less to be received in part, than in the whole, but in each of them the whole body of our Saviour Jesu Christ." The importance of the 1549 Communion service is that it proves how slowly Cranmer moved from the structure of the ancient rites except under compelling conviction, and at the same time the greatness of his liturgical genius. All that has vanished from the medieval rite is the Invocation of saints, some of the ceremonial, notably the Fraction and Commixture, the complexity of its musical items—Gradual, Alleluia and Sequence, Offertory, and Communion—and the prayers said silently. What is added is an immense enrichment. Order is restored to the strangely dislocated Consecration Prayer of the Roman rite, and to it is added an invocation of the Holy Spirit suggested by the Greek Liturgy of St Basil. The rite retained an "*anamnesis*", or remembrance of Christ "having in remembrance His blessed passion, mighty resurrection and glorious ascension", the total removal of which, in 1552, certainly impoverishes the Anglican rite.

But though capable of interpretation as the expression of reformed doctrine, the rite of 1549 did not satisfy the more radical reformers, and was only acceptable to the "catholic" party when interpreted in the sense which Cranmer himself repudiated. The second Prayer

Book of 1552 was therefore an unequivocal document. Even Cranmer was now convinced that much more drastic steps were necessary. Some of these have been already noticed in our survey of the historical development, but as now we survey the rite as a whole the old Sarum structure is seen to be broken up. The Commandments are introduced, as in Continental rites, and the Kyries turned into responses. The Prayer for the Church, significantly without any mention of the dead, is given a new place after the offertory which, despite the absence of liturgical precedent, was retained in 1928. The preparation of the communicants (invitation, confession, and absolution, Comfortable Words) follows immediately in order that Communion shall follow directly the words of institution. Similarly the Prayer of Humble Access breaks the sequence of Preface, Sanctus, and Canon, liturgically without precedent, but transferred of set purpose because consecration is now essentially the prelude to Communion which, as the true centre of gravity of the whole rite, follows it immediately. The transference of the Prayer of Oblation so as to follow communion removed all sacrificial language from the context of the elements: its deeper theological significance has already been noticed. This arrangement had the marked disadvantage that it made the prayer of thanksgiving a mere alternative, still a defect in the service. Finally, the *Gloria in Excelsis* is moved to the end of the service, which thus ends on a note of triumphant praise. It is this 1552 rite which is substantially that of our present book of Common Prayer, and it demonstrates to what lengths Cranmer was prepared to go to give expression to doctrinal change, once he was thoroughly convinced, as by 1550 he was.

The methods employed in the making of the Prayer Book having been illustrated from the rites, or services, a brief survey of ceremonial changes may be added. The stages of change are well exemplified by the Ordinal. The *traditio instrumentorum*, the gift of the symbols of ministry for the priesthood in the Sarum rite consisted of the chalice and paten with prepared wine and hosts, the perfect symbol of sacrificial priesthood. In 1549 the priest was given the Bible in one hand and the chalice, with the bread, in the other, the ministry of the word and sacraments being thus symbolized. In 1552 the Bible only is given: the ministry is still the ministry of the word and sacraments, but the sacraments are dependent on the word. In general, however, ceremonial was reduced to a bare minimum. In the baptismal office, for example, the old ceremonial was considerably reduced in 1549 when the gift of salt and the anointing with saliva were removed from the rites of the Catechumenate, which still, however, took place at the church door and was thus marked off from Baptism. The blessing of the font was still a separate rite performed at least monthly, but without the use of oil and with the Sign of the Cross only. At the Baptism itself the gift of the taper was discarded, but the anointing and vesting with the white baptismal robe remained. In 1552 only the Sign of the Cross at Baptism itself remained of all the wealth of medieval ceremonial. The font was not blessed and even the threefold immersion in the name of the Trinity vanished. Most of these omissions were suggested by Bucer's *Censura*. The more extreme reformers would, indeed, have removed all ceremonial, and the Puritans of the seventeenth century strenuously opposed even the use of the Sign of the Cross in Baptism and of the ring in marriage as superstitious. If any principle is to be discerned in this virtual abolition of all ceremonies it is probably to be found in reliance upon the sole validity and efficacy of the word, from which ceremonial might seem to detract; but judging from Puritan protests the desire to make a clean cut with Rome and all its ways was the dominant motive. Bucer wrote of the first Prayer Book that concessions had been made "both to a respect for antiquity and to the infirmity of the present age". The later Puritan certainly had little respect for antiquity, and was not prepared to make concessions to human infirmity.

We may conclude our survey by a final analysis of the essential difference between the method of Cranmer and that of the more extreme reformers both on the Continent and in this country. Cranmer's ideal was a rite both catholic and reformed; catholic in that it did not discard the heritage of fifteen centuries of Church life, reformed because medieval accretions and distortions were cut away, the criterion being that nothing was to be ordained or allowed contrary to Holy Scripture. On the other hand those whose sympathies lay with Geneva and Zürich sought to establish scriptural rights without reference to existing forms. In England conflict with the Puritans was only brought to an end with the Restoration of Charles II, when the Puritans left the Church of England, having failed at the

Savoy Conference to achieve their desired reforms. Under the Caroline Divines the spirit of Cranmer prevailed and the Prayer Book, passed by the Convocations and annexed as a schedule to the Caroline Act of Uniformity, remained essentially Cranmer's work. This, however, does not mean that there had been no development during the hundred years since Cranmer's second Prayer Book. The Puritan conflict had produced a "high-church" party within the Church of England, many of whom, as the Scottish Prayer Book of 1637 shows, would have been happier with 1549 than with 1552. Their influence, dominant in the reign of Charles II, was partly lost by the secession in 1690 of the Nonjurors (one Archbishop, six bishops, and four hundred clergy), but such attempts as were made to achieve reconciliation with the Nonconformists came to nothing. The Book of 1662 remained the Prayer Book of the Church of England to our own day.

6

The Background of Liturgical Change 1662–1965

BETWEEN 1662 and 1965 the only legal change in the uniform use of the Prayer Book was the Act of Uniformity Amendment Act of 1872 which allowed the use of a shortened form of Morning and Evening Prayer in parish churches on weekdays and the production of new services provided they consisted only of Prayer Book material with hymns. Yet those three centuries saw the Evangelical movement of the eighteenth and early nineteenth centuries, to be followed by the Oxford Movement, both of them profoundly changing the thought and the devotion of Anglican churchmen. If the former renewed the spiritual life of the Church and deepened individual piety, the latter produced a new respect for the continuity of the Church's life and a new concern for seemly worship with the revival of ceremonial. The leaders of the Oxford Movement, indeed, went beyond the teaching and claims of the Caroline Divines while their successors not only borrowed their ceremonial from Rome but extremists used Roman rites. It is a tragedy that this should have led not only to controversy but to recourse to the Courts of Law for redress. By the end of the century it was clear that the principle of uniformity was no longer accepted and a Royal Commission reported in 1906 that "the law of public worship in the Church of England is too narrow for the religious life of the present generation. It needlessly condemns much which a great section of church people, including many of her most devoted members, value; and modern thought and feeling are characterized by a care for ceremonial, a sense of dignity in worship and an appreciation of the continuity of the church, which were not similarly felt at the time when the law took its present shape." But it also listed a series of "practices of special gravity and significance", nearly all borrowings from Rome, which should be made to cease; and since "the machinery for discipline has broken down" this should be strengthened.

This is the background to the proposals for Prayer Book revision passed by Convocations and the Church Assembly but finally rejected by Parliament in 1928. Controversy, apart from the proposal to allow carefully phrased prayers for the dead, centred round the proposal to allow the reservation of the sacrament for the communion of the sick, and the changes in the Holy Communion service. Basically this was a return to 1549 but with the Invocation of the Holy Spirit transferred so as to follow the Words of Institution. This alienated both Anglo-Catholics and Evangelicals, while others disliked the whole process of "legalization" as a disguised instrument of discipline to cause extremist practices to cease. It was clear that reform must be achieved in other ways, but the Bishops allowed the "Deposited Book" to be used where desired, since the Convocations and the Church Assembly had approved it. It should be noted that the proposal had never been to replace the Prayer Book of 1662 but to provide a legal alternative. The necessity for a new flexibility, however, remained and was strengthened in the next forty years both by historical and sociological change and by theological and liturgical insights which we must now examine.

First, it is not generally realized that in the forty years between 1920 and 1960 over a third of the population of this country has been rehoused, and in some of the great cities the proportion has been higher. Great housing estates have come into being, requiring new churches to serve a population with changing social habits. Here has grown up a new liturgical tradition based neither on 8 o'clock plain celebration nor on 11 o'clock High Mass, but on Parish Communion at 9 or 9.30. This has meant the widespread disappearance of Sunday Mattins, and Evensong also has declined with the growth of transport and a changed attitude to Sunday.

Parallel with this growth of new housing, the population dispersed from the older town areas has been replaced by new inhabitants or the area has been redeveloped with flats. Again church life has taken on a new look: congregations shrink, new methods of pastoral care have to be tried, even churchmanship changes. Finally, as every parish priest is aware, there is in the second half of the twentieth century a new mobility of the whole population. Few are able to settle down in one congregation for more than a few years and violent changes in rite or ceremonial encountered in a new neighbourhood are resented. All these factors have created a new situation in which thinking men are prepared to examine the possibilities of change.

But, secondly, there has been theological change which has in great measure cut across, or undercut, the barriers of churchmanship, and indeed of denomination. Partly this is the result of the growth of a secular civilization which has no use for worship and which has forced Christians to see that what they hold in common is infinitely more important than their differences. Partly there is a new concern for the secular with the realization that God is the God of all life as well as the Lord of history, and that "concern for life" must replace the old divisions into the sacred and the secular. If this is true, then liturgical worship must be bound up with, and must express, God's concern and therefore ours: it must reach men where they are; and therefore its content and its forms must be meaningful. And yet liturgy must still embody God's revelation of himself in Christ and be the vehicle of worship which is not only in spirit but in truth.

To this we must add the insights both theological and liturgical which have affected all the Churches through the liturgical movement. Within the Church of Rome this has meant the use of the vernacular, the insistence on the congregation "praying the Mass" and not praying at the Mass and therefore a new emphasis on audibility. More important is the restoration of communion within the Mass as an essential of the rite and a new stress on the importance of the ministry of the Word. Even more important is the recognition that the celebrant acts as the representative of the whole body of the faithful, that the whole service, including the Canon, is a corporate act and the offering not primarily that of the priest but of the Body of Christ. In many of these respects the Church of Rome is recovering what are essentially Reformation insights, but insights which within the Churches of the Reformation, including the Church of England, have often been neglected or, in practice, obscured. Cranmer, indeed, intended to restore the communion of the people as of primary importance to the understanding of the Eucharist and his liturgical reconstruction is shaped to that end. But it proved impossible to change the devotional habits of a population conditioned by the medieval practice of non-communicating attendance. The seventeenth and eighteenth centuries were content with a monthly communion. The Evangelicals, with their emphasis on personal piety, began the practice of early morning communion, to which the Tractarians added High Mass, with communion for the aged and the the sick. But only in our own day, since the 1930s, have the sociological, corporate implications of the liturgy been widely accepted by Anglicans, largely through the impact of A. G. Hebert's *Liturgy and Society*. As a result the Parish and People movement has drawn together in a new understanding Anglicans of differing churchmanship and has fostered the Parish Communion as the focus of the Church's worship. But this fresh understanding of the meaning and importance of liturgy is universal, and not merely Roman and Anglican. Some of the most significant work in the field of scholarship has been done by Lutheran and Reformed churchmen. The Church of Scotland has undertaken the revision of its own liturgy and their representatives with those of the Episcopal Church meet regularly with the representatives of the Church of England, the Free Churches and the Church of Rome in a Joint Liturgical Group. Meanwhile in South India a new liturgy, produced by churchmen with widely varying backgrounds, has won wide acclaim. If then we survey Western Christendom what becomes clear is that from the standpoint of liturgy we have all passed out of the Middle Ages. In so far as the Reformation was a reaction against medieval deformations its work has been done, the battle has been won. Its emphasis on the primary importance of the Bible has been accepted and the characteristic Anglican appeal to the early Church has, in the field of liturgy, assumed a wholly new importance. To this we must now turn.

The immense labours of scholars in this century have transformed the extent of our knowledge, and there is now agreement over a wide field. To quote the memorandum *Prayer Book Revision in the Church of England* (1957), "We know now, in a way that was not realized in

1928, that the Eucharist has developed directly out of Jewish forms of thanksgiving, that the first Christians thought of consecration as effected by thanksgiving, and that controversies between Eastern and Western views of consecration (which played a great part in the debates on the Revised Prayer Book) belong to a later, not to the earliest period." Thus it can now be taken for granted that our Lord, in the Upper Room, blessed God over the bread and wine, and though we do not know the words of his blessing, but only the significance which they gave—this is my body, this is my blood—we recognize that the blessing, or thanksgiving, was the heart of his action and so must be of ours. Much work, too, has been done on the meaning of *anamnesis*, the word for remembrance or memorial, and though interpretations still differ, we all know that it does not mean a subjective act of recollection bound up with receiving communion, but the corporate act of the Church, bound up with the thanksgiving as well as the communion. Or again, whatever our background of churchmanship, we all recognize that the essential pattern of the Eucharist follows from our Lord's action in the upper room, when he took, and blessed, and broke, and gave. And we "do this" in and through him to the glory of the Father.

When, therefore, the Archbishops in 1955 appointed a Liturgical Commission to prepare for revision of the Prayer Book the change from the 1920s both in church life and in liturgical scholarship was considerable. Evangelicals and Anglo-Catholics had learnt much from one another and both were facing widespread change in social habit. But parallel with the work of the Commission the Convocations were continuing their work on Canon Law. The old controversy over vestments and the interpretation of the Ornaments Rubric had lost its virulence, and the new Canons accepted all the existing uses. Most important of all, the Prayer Book (Alternative and Other Services) Measure, passed in 1965, gave the Church freedom for liturgical experiment: the way was open to go forward. Unfortunately the proposal for a national Synod, of bishops, clergy, and laity, was delayed, and the work of liturgical revision had to be carried through not only in two Convocations but by reference to the House of Laity of the Church Assembly, which had power of veto but not of amendment. This complicated the procedure and delayed the final acceptance of the services, but in 1967 authorized experiment began.

It is of first importance to recognize the significance of the proposal to proceed by experiment with the consent of the parishes. This procedure rested on the conviction that the worth and acceptability of services can only be judged by using them. Moreover, if the experiment was to be worthwhile it meant providing a series of choices, and seeming untidiness could not be avoided. But the choice was deliberately made not to impose one invariable form but to give the maximum freedom of choice. It was for the same reason that rubrical directions were kept to a minimum, and regarding place and posture none was given; thus the parishes could work out their ceremonial according to customary use. But the Commission was also aware that differences in church architecture also demanded this freedom. One of the problems of the Church of England since the Reformation has been how to use for congregational worship medieval churches where it mattered little if people could hear, since the services were in Latin. The Prayer Books originally provided that communicants should move to the chancel, and for some years the communion table could, alternatively, be moved to the chancel step. But when, after Laud's reforms, it became obligatory to rail the altar and customary to restore it to its medieval position against the east wall, neither the Reformation use of the clergy standing to the north and south of the Holy Table, nor the eastward position adopted by Tractarians, dealt with the isolation of the clergy removed from their congregation by a long English chancel and sometimes a central tower as well. For the period of experiment, therefore, wisdom lay in giving freedom to experiment. There is no reason why, for the whole service, the celebrant should stand at the altar, no reason why the altar should not be moved so that the people of God should gather round the Table of the Lord; and there is ancient precedent for the celebrant facing the congregation. It is equally true that the early Church stood for the thanksgiving, and there is both ancient and Reformation precedent for standing to receive communion. No doubt long-established habits of devotion will not easily be changed, nor need they be, but the way is open to discover what is best.

The services for liturgical experiment are discussed in subsequent chapters. Here it is sufficient to point out that they are published with the somewhat unhelpful titles of First and Second Series. The First Series gives legal authority to the services of 1928 with some modification where judged desirable. The Report of 1965, introducing the Series, said: "They embody variants from the Book of Common Prayer which are already used in many churches. They were the result of long consideration by the Bishops, and of consultation with some members of the Liturgical Commission and of the Joint Liturgical Standing Committee of the Convocations of Canterbury and York." The Second Series consists of new services which, unlike 1928, are not modifications of 1662. Indeed, when the Liturgical Commission was re-formed in 1962 one of the tasks laid on it by the archbishops was "a radical consideration of the eucharistic rite". The service of 1967—and by this title it will be referred to in subsequent chapters—forms no part of the series 1549, 1552, 1662, 1928, but, as was suggested by the 1958 Lambeth Conference, goes behind the Reformation controversies so far as this is possible and is based on our understanding of the early Church and our own needs in the twentieth century.

PART TWO

THE CONTENTS
OF THE ENGLISH
PRAYER BOOK

6

The Holy Communion

CRANMER'S intention, as we have seen was the abolition of the sacrificial rite of the Middle Ages and the restoration of Communion as its essential content. This is reflected in the title of the service. In the first Prayer Book the word Mass still appeared as a sub-title: "The supper of the Lord, and the Holy Communion commonly called the Mass", but in 1552 the present title appeared, and has never been altered. The service is therefore a service of commemoration, the Lord's Supper, and a service of fellowship with our Lord in his death and resurrection, the Holy Communion. To emphasize this communion aspect, non-communicating attendance was forbidden until 1662, when the rubric was omitted because the practice had ceased. The same emphasis appears in the Communion of the Sick, where the opening rubric still provides that three, or two at least, shall communicate with the sick person.

The last rubric before the service is also a serious attempt to make the service truly congregational. A characteristic feature of the English parish church is its long chancel. This did not greatly matter in the Middle Ages when it was not necessary to hear what was said, and Communion was infrequent. In 1549 the worshippers came into the quire at the offertory, each making his offering into the poor men's box. "Then as many as shall be partakers of the Holy Communion, shall tarry still in the quire—or nigh the quire. All other— shall depart out of the quire, except the Ministers and Clerks." Otherwise the celebrant stood, as always in the Middle Ages, before the altar and wore an alb with a vestment (chasuble) or cope. This arrangement was abandoned in 1552. By this time the stone altar had given place to a movable wooden table, and our present rubric allows it to stand in the body of the church or in the chancel. In many places it became customary to move it in Communion time to the chancel step, but whether moved or not the intention is to make this service the service of the Church which all may hear and share (being communicants) and not a rite performed far off by a priest on their behalf. Further, in 1552, the minister is directed to stand at the north side. Ingenious attempts have been made to explain this rubric other than in its plain sense. But Lancelot Andrewes is but commenting quaintly on normal Anglican practice when he speaks of the ministers at the Holy Table "the one at the one end, the other at the other, representing the two Cherubims at the mercy seat". The real purpose of the change of position was that the congregation might have the holy table in full view. It was Laud who placed the Communion-tables altar-wise and insisted that rails, hitherto unusual, should always be provided. Even so, until very recently, several churches possessed Communion-tables set in the midst of the chancel and railed on four sides. The eastward position has been re-introduced since the Oxford movement, and held to be legal provided that the manual acts are visible to the congregation.

The medieval rite proper really opened with the note of praise. The only remnant of the ancient introductory litany was the Kyrie, itself sung like the Introit, but both led on to the *Gloria in Excelsis* which preceded the Collect. In 1549 the only change was that what had been part of the private preparation of the celebrant, the Lord's prayer and Collect for purity, were said audibly so as to include the congregation, and the service still opens in this way. In 1552, however, the Ten Commandments were introduced as the communicants' preparation, the Kyrie being transferred into a response. The note of penitence thus became dominant, and the *Gloria* being out of place was moved to its present position. The permissive alternative of 1928, our Lord's Summary of the Law, though in some ways more suitable, leaves the service with no significant reference to the Old Testament.[1] The re-introduction of a prophetic lection, chosen to fit the season of the Church's year, permitted in 1967, has everything to recommend it. Then, provided that Confirmation

[1] The early liturgies contained a "prophetic lection" which still survives at Toledo in the Mozarabic rite.

candidates were taught properly to prepare for Communion, the substitution of the Kyrie for the Ten Commandments would not be a serious loss.

The service then moved on to the Collect for the day, which was, until 1662, followed, and not preceded, by the Collect for the King. Several rites of the Anglican family, the Scottish, the South African, the English book of 1928, and the Irish (permissibly) omit the Collect for the King here, since the monarch is prayed for in the great intercession fo the Church militant. Its introduction at this point was understandable in Tudor England, but hardly defensible to-day. The Collect, Epistle, and Gospel for the day are all that remain of the "Proper" of the Mass, the elements which varied from Sunday to Sunday and marked the course of the Christian year. This ancient "Proper" included Psalms like the Introit, at the beginning, the Gradual sung between the Epistle and the Gospel, the offertory and the Communion at the end. Originally they were complete Psalms, or substantial portions of them, but in course of time they became both shorter and set to more and more complicated musical settings, and for this reason were omitted in the English Prayer Book. The Proper also included three collects, the Collect for the Day, Secret, and Post-Communion of which only the first remains, and of course the lessons, Epistle and Gospel.

This liturgy of the Word, represented in its fullness in the early liturgies of the Church, and including one or more lessons from the Old Testament, is an essential part of the service, for in it is set forth, throughout the Christian year, the saving acts of God. This is what, in any one season, is the Word of God to man, the ground of his faith and the inspiration for life. And, in general, it is true that the Epistles and Gospels of the English rite go back to the most ancient lectionaries we possess, those of the sixth to the eighth centuries. The Gospel, as the Word of the Lord, is reverenced by the congregation standing to hear it, and was formerly dignified by the Gospel procession with lights. This use of light, though doubtless in origin utilitarian, was beautiful and appropriate as symbolizing the light of the Gospel shining in the darkness. The Creed which now follows the lections was not officially adopted at Rome until the eleventh century, but in Gallican countries is found four centuries earlier, and in the East as early as the beginning of the sixth century. It is a fitting conclusion to the lections, for it proclaims the whole gospel of which they are the portions for the day. In contrast to the proper chants the invariant chants were always sung to simple tunes, and the Creed had commonly only one setting down to the time of the Reformation.[1] As soon as the English rite appeared, appropriate and simple musical settings (on Cranmer's principle of one syllable to a note) were produced by John Merbecke, who in 1550 issued "The Booke of Common Praier Noted".[2] Our present rubric, "And the Gospel ended shall be sung or said the Creed", still suggests that the Creed should normally be sung, though the second Prayer Book had directed it to be said.

Finally in "the liturgy of the Word" comes the sermon. As we have seen, a sermon has from the days of the Apostles been an integral part of the Lord's Supper. In the narrative of Acts when the Church at Troas was gathered in the evening to break bread St Paul preached until midnight. Justin Martyr tells how the President instructs and encourages the people to practise the truths contained in the Scripture lections, and in the fourth century at Antioch every priest had the right to preach before the bishop's sermon. In the Middle Ages the sermon had fallen on evil days, but was popular where it could be had. It can hardly be doubted that from the seventeenth century onward, if not from the sixteenth, the sermon became of central importance in the life of the English Church, but unfortunately divorced from the Lord's Supper which is its ancient and rightful place. The Prayer Books of Edward the Sixth's reign suggest the reading of one of the Homilies (see Note 4) designed to teach reformed doctrine, "and for stay of such errors as were then by ignorant preachers sparkled among the people", and the reference still remains. The use of the sermon for purely controversial purposes led more than once to its suppression with the substitution of a homily. With the sermon the liturgy of the Word is brought to a close and the "liturgy of the Upper Room" begins. In the history of the English rite the break has, however, been made after the offertory, or after the prayer for the Church militant. Thus prayers are provided at the

[1] This is disputed, but see Frere, *A New History of the Book of Common Prayer*, p. 464.

[2] Merbecke was himself a reformed Churchman and in 1543 narrowly escaped the stake. His offence was the construction of an English Concordance to the Bible.

end of the service to be said after the offertory when there is no Communion, and these are followed by a rubric which directs that on Sundays and other holy days (if there be no Communion), the service shall be said as far as the prayer for the Church militant with one or more of these Collects added. The insertion of Sundays into this rubric in 1662 is the first Prayer Book recognition that a Sunday might pass without a full celebration of the sacrament.

The Offertory, however, essentially belongs to the "liturgy of the Upper Room", for it is the people's offering, originally not only of bread and wine but of oil, cheese, vegetables, fruit, and flowers, the freewill offering of Christians both for the Lord's Supper and for the needs of their poorer brethren. The bread and the wine were, however, in a special sense the Christian sacrifice, as St Ireraeus says, and with the offering of them the Eucharist proper begins. The Psalm sung during the people's offering remained during the Middle Ages as "the Offertory" and the Collect called the Secret often preserved the original language of offering. Thus the secret for the Fifth Sunday after Pentecost[1] reads, "Hearken, O Lord, to our prayers and graciously accept these offerings of thy servants and handmaids: that what individuals have offered to the honour of thy name, may avail unto all for salvation." In course of time the offering of gifts became a money offering, and the connection with the bread and wine only indirect. The rubrics at the end of the 1549 book provide that the families of the parish shall in turn offer every Sunday, at the time of the Offertory, the just value and price of the holy loaf, and shall also send a member or representative to receive Communion. "And by this means the minister, having always some to communicate with him, may accordingly solemnize so high and holy mysteries." This interesting provision vanished in 1552 when the curate and churchwardens were to provide the bread and wine at the expense of the parish.

The Offertory then became the offering of "alms and oblations", "alms" for the poor and "oblations" for other purposes, notably the support of the ministry.[2] This, as Bishop Dowden has shown, accounts for the character of the Offertory sentences. In 1549 the

[1] Quoted from Hebert, *Liturgy and Society*, p. 77.
[2] Cf. the 1549 rubric, "And at the offering days appointed, every man and woman shall pay to the curate the due and accustomed offerings."

worshippers came into the quire and offered personally into the poor men's box, and in some places a second box was provided for oblations. Historically therefore the word oblation in the English Prayer Book, unlike the Scottish, has no reference to the bread and wine which anciently was the primary reference. There is no reason doctrinally why the old connection of the word should not be restored, and the bread and wine, made once again the people's offering, presented at the Lord's Table by representatives of the congregation. Such a restoration of the Offertory to its primitive significance would be both Catholic and Evangelical. The 1928 book strangely made no suggestion, but was content to insert a new offertory sentence "Melchezedek King of Salem brought forth bread and wine; and he was priest of the most high God", which without exegesis might even be misleading. The collection of alms in a decent basin and the humble presentation of them, together with the placing of the bread and wine upon the table were inserted in 1662 from the Scottish Prayer Book of 1637. The Scottish book had "offer up and place" with reference to the elements but, though proposed for adoption, the words "offer up" were rejected by Convocation. In passing it may be noticed that the English Prayer Book does not, since 1549, allow a mixed chalice. The practice of using water with wine at the Holy Communion is, however, traceable to the earliest days; it is, in fact, the normal custom of Eastern peoples to drink wine diluted with water. It was only later that the mixed chalice was given a symbolic meaning.

In 1549 the heart of the rite, the ancient *anaphora*, followed immediately upon the Offertory, with *Sursum corda*, Preface, *Sanctus* and long Consecration Prayer, which began with the great intercession—the prayer for the whole state of Christ's Church. At that time the preparation for Communion followed the consecration, with the invitation to "draw near and take this holy Sacrament". As we have already seen, this liturgically almost perfect sequence was broken in 1552, and has never been restored, even in 1928. The doctrinal reason for its dislocation we have already discussed, but in addition we may notice that devotionally this very long prayer is difficult to follow with sufficient concentration, which probably accounts for the reluctance of the 1928 revisers to restore it. The great intercession has no fixed place in the ancient liturgies, but the Mass of the Faithful normally began with intercessory prayer and there is thus ancient precedent, if such were required, for the placing of the prayer for the Church where it has now stood since 1552, and where it was still placed in the Prayer Book of 1928. As it stood in 1552 the prayer, despite its opening phrase: "to make prayers and supplications, and to give thanks, for all men", contained no thanksgiving. This was due to the shortening of the prayer in the second Prayer Book by the omission of the praise and thanksgiving for the saints and the final prayer for the departed: this last omission being emphasized by the addition of the words "militant here in earth" to the invitation "Let us pray for the whole state of Christ's Church". In 1662 this was remedied by the addition of thanksgiving "for all thy servants departed this life in thy faith and fear". The order of the prayer in which kings and those in authority precede the ministry of the Church is probably based on 1 Timothy 2.1, which provides the prayer with its opening phrases. "I exhort, therefore, that, first of all, supplications, prayers, intercessions, and giving of thanks be made for all men: for kings, and for all that are in authority, that we may lead a quiet and peaceable life in all godliness and honesty." But whatever its inspiration the Church's prayer for the world is part of her essential work. For the Church is a royal priesthood; it stands between God and the world, on the one hand with the priestly ministry of the Gospel (compare Rom. 15.16) and on the other with the priestly ministry of intercession. The 1928 Prayer Book therefore, rightly, does not restrict the Church's intercession to Christian kings, princes and governors, but prays for all nations and all kings and rulers. In the early liturgies the intercession with which the prayers of the faithful began was general: the prayer for the Church was separate, and placed either within the consecration prayer or in its preface. Our present prayer, restricted to those who profess the faith is, as its title makes clear, the prayer for the Church. In 1928 it becomes a more general intercession which includes the world, thus combining the two prayers of the early church services. It could well be argued that the restoration of the Litany as the introduction to the Communion Service would provide the general intercession without which any Lord's Supper is really incomplete.

When there were no communicants the Prayer for the Church militant is followed, as we have seen, by "Table Prayers", as they came to be called. But normally it was to be followed by the exhortation and preparation for Communion. The history of the exhortations is complicated, but they need not concern us, for to-day they have virtually ceased to be part of the Communion service. We come, then, to the immediate preparation for Communion which goes back to 1548 when provision was made for Communion within the framework of the Latin Mass. In 1549 this section of the service was still placed after the Consecration Prayer. But once the Communion of the people was, so to speak, placed at the heart of the Consecration Prayer itself, the preparation most naturally preceded the prayer; it has stood in its present place since 1552, and is left there in 1928 and in 1967.

The invitation summarizes the exhortation with the reminder that repentance, love, obedience, and faith are the requirements of all who would receive the sacrament. It was the Christian love here insisted upon which in the ancient services was expressed by the kiss of peace. The repentance leads naturally to the confession which, though owing something to the medieval form, is an adaptation by Cranmer from the longer form in Hermann's *Consultation*. The absolution is from the same source, but also follows closely the Sarum form. The provision of a form of confession and absolution in the service itself made private confession unnecessary except, as provided in the first exhortation, for those who cannot quiet their own consciences, but require further comfort or counsel. The Prayer Book makes it clear that compulsory auricular confession is required of no man, but that it is available for all who need it. What, in any case, the Anglican reformers again following Hermann have done, and this is a truly reformed emphasis, is to add to the absolution the comfortable words which add the seal of God's Word to the absolution pronounced by the minister.

It is at this point that contact is again made with the Communion Services of the primitive Church, where the heart of the service, the *Anaphora*, begins. We have already seen that the exhortation "Lift up your hearts" with the people's response is found as early as the beginning of the second century, and is included in all the rites known to us. What, however, is far more important than liturgical antiquity is that worship at this point is explicitly united with the worship of the whole Church, with the worship of heaven itself, with angels and archangels and all the company of heaven, leading on to the *Sanctus*, itself based on Isaiah's vision in the Temple. This Preface in the East is invariant throughout the year, and in it the whole course of God's self-revelation in the Old Testament is proclaimed with praise and thanksgiving leading up to redemption through our Lord Jesus Christ which is the subject of the *anamnesis*, or memorial, of the Consecration Prayer proper. But our service is essentially a Western rite, and here the Preface is a framework within which Proper Prefaces, that is commemorations for the great feasts of the Church's year, are included. Our Prayer Book provides for five: Christmas, Easter, Ascension, Whitsuntide, and Trinity, whereas Sarum had ten. It has been widely recognized that a fuller Proper is desirable, and nearly all the services of the English family provide it. The book proposed in 1928, for example, provides for Epiphany, Maundy Thursday, Eastertide, and Ascensiontide, as well as for the feasts of the Presentation of Christ, the Annunciation and Transfiguration, and Saints' Days.

The *Sanctus* has from the earliest days been said or sung by the people, and previous to 1552 was followed by the *Hosanna* and *Benedictus*: "Blessed be he that cometh in the name of the Lord." This, however, seemed to suggest a doctrine of the real presence, and the chant was therefore shortened so as to include only a paraphrase of the *Hosanna*, which was attached to the *Sanctus*: "Glory be to Thee, O Lord most high." Following the *Sanctus* it was universal to go on directly to the Consecration Prayer, known in the Middle Ages as the Canon. The Prayer of Humble Access said after the Consecration and before Communion, as it was in the 1549 service, was said by Bishop Gardiner to teach the doctrine of the real presence, and therefore in 1552 it was moved to its present place and its wording slightly altered.[1]

We come, then, to the Prayer of Consecration. The title "Prayer of Consecration" is derived from the Scottish Prayer Book of 1637 and was inserted in 1662.

The essential fact about consecration in the English service is that it is a prayer. The Continental reformers generally placed at the

---

[1] 1549 read, "Grant us . . . so to eat the flesh of Thy dear Son Jesus Christ and to drink His blood in these holy mysteries."

heart of the service the narrative of our Lord's institution of the sacrament standing somewhat apart from the accompanying prayer. The English service has at its heart the prayer "Hear us, O merciful Father, we most humbly beseech thee, and grant that we receiving these thy creatures of bread and wine, according to thy Son our Saviour Jesus Christ's holy institution, in remembrance of His death and passion, may be partakers of His most blessed body and blood." This prayer is not an explicit prayer for the consecration of the elements, which is its essential difference from 1549, but a prayer for the gift of the heavenly realities to those who receive. It avoids all "theories" of consecration whether by the words of institution, as in later Western theology, or by the invocation of the Spirit as in the East. Cranmer, indeed, introduced an invocation of the Spirit into the first Prayer Book, but insisted that its wording—"that they (the elements) may be unto us the Body and Blood"—meant only that "in the godly using of them they be unto the receivers Christ's body and blood". He removed it when he found that it was interpreted differently. The Prayer Book, properly understood, has therefore no "moment of consecration". It must, moreover, be remembered that from 1552 to 1662 there were no "manual acts" for which provision is now made by indented rubrics. Cranmer in 1549 had directed the priest to take the bread and the cup into his hands during the narrative of the institution, and to break the bread at the administration. These rubrics, omitted in 1552, were restored by the Caroline Divines but with the significant change that the priest is to break the bread and lay his hands on the cup at the recital of the words of institution, thus re-enacting what our Lord did in the Upper Room. The change is not without significance, and makes it possible to shift the emphasis from the petition of the prayer to the words of institution. Not all English churchmen in the sixteenth and seventeenth centuries shared Cranmer's eucharistic theology.

The second important fact about the English Consecration Prayer is that it has neither oblation of the elements, the heart of the sacrifice of the Mass, nor memorial before God. The oblation had already disappeared in 1549, but the words "we thy humble servants do celebrate and make here before thy divine Majesty, with these thy holy gifts, the memorial which thy Son hath willed us to make", still pleaded before God the one perfect and finished sacrifice of

Christ. There is an all-important distinction between offering a sacrifice and pleading a sacrifice, and many Anglicans of the seventeenth and eighteenth centuries, including Charles Wesley,[1] did, in their devotion at Holy Communion, thus plead Christ's death. The Evangelical churchman to-day could, indeed, use the words of 1549, since the all-sufficiency of Christ's sacrifice once offered is explicitly safeguarded by that rite. We do make the memorial which our Lord willed us to make and in the sight of God, for his sacrifice is our right of access to the Father. But "Do this" does not mean "Offer this" nor does *anamnesis* mean a memorial offering to God. We cannot offer Christ, but we must be united with him in his death and resurrection and we offer ourselves "in him and through him". The whole Consecration Prayer therefore "proclaims the Lord's death till he come" and leads directly to the Communion which follows immediately the Words of Institution (even without an Amen till one was inserted in 1662). The real Amen of the 1552 service comes at the end of the Lord's Prayer. There is no point in asserting that the English Consecration Prayer is perfect, and later we must assess the possibilities of revision, but its intention is perfectly clear, and that intention it achieves.

The words of administration of the sacrament are, however, an admitted compromise, for they are the combination, made in 1559, of the forms both of 1549 and 1552. That the 1549 form, "The body of our Lord Jesus Christ which was given for thee, preserve thy body and soul unto everlasting life", is in itself and by itself evangelical is shown by Baxter's Savoy Liturgy in which the words were even strengthened, "This is the Body of Christ which is given for thee." Our Lord said, "This is my body", "This is my blood", and Baxter was only reproducing his words more exactly. The form of 1552, "Take and eat this in remembrance that Christ died for thee and feed on Him in thy heart by faith with thanksgiving", does make clear that reception is by faith, but leaves unsaid the words with which our Lord himself gave the bread and wine to his disciples. It has, further, the grave demerit that it concentrates the thought of the worshipper on the action of receiving rather than upon the Lord's in giving. The present combined form, however inconvenient when there are many communicants, has the merit that its primary emphasis is upon the

[1] As for example in his hymn "Victim Divine, thy grace we claim".

75

self-giving of the Lord while the demands upon the worshipper, faith, and remembrance are explicitly stated.

After the Lord's Prayer, which marks the focus of the service, come the alternative Prayers of Oblation and Thanksgiving. The first has already been commented upon, and its position theologically justified. It stresses the relation of the worshippers present to the whole Church and thus emphasizes the essentially corporate character of the whole service. In 1549, when this prayer still formed part of the Canon, the Prayer of Thanksgiving followed the *Agnus Dei*, sung during Communion, and the Post-communion sentence, both of which were abolished in 1552, and immediately preceded the Blessing. From 1552 onwards it became an alternative to the Prayer of Oblation, and preceded the transferred *Gloria in Excelsis*. This can only be regarded as a serious flaw in the Anglican rite. Both oblation and thanksgiving are essential parts of the service, and the relation of the sacrament to the daily life of fellowship and witness is an important emphasis which ought not to be omitted. At the risk of lengthening unduly the Post-communion, both prayers should surely be said, or the two combined.

The *Gloria*, retained in its present position in the 1928 book, is a fitting climax to the service. Originally it was a Greek hymn for Mattins dating at least as far back as the fourth century, and first came into the Western liturgy most suitably in the Christmas Mass. It only came into general use, however, in the eleventh century as the opening hymn of praise in the liturgy. It has been often pointed out that the narrative of the Lord's Supper in the gospels ends with the singing of a hymn, and the transference of the *Gloria* to a like place in the Lord's Supper has a peculiar felicity.

The Blessing, customary throughout the Middle Ages but not prescribed in the Missal, is the second part of the Prayer Book form. The first, taken from Philippians 4.7, goes back to the little English Communion order of 1548. The full form has been used since 1549. Its special point peculiar to the English service is that it carries forward into life the blessing of the Eucharist, "The peace of God, which passes all understanding, *keep* your hearts and minds in the knowledge and love of God, and of His Son Jesus Christ our Lord."

If now we turn to the alternative services proposed in this century it is convenient to confine ourselves to First and Second Series, since

First Series embodies the revision of 1928 in a fully authoritative form.

The *First Series* order retains the general structure of 1662. After the Lord's Prayer and the Collect for Purity, the Ten Commandments (or our Lord's summary of the Law) and the Kyries are provided as alternatives. An Old Testament lesson can precede the reading of the Epistle and Gospel—a wise addition in days when Anglicans often attend only the Eucharist on Sunday. Then follows the Creed, and "then may follow the Sermon". The Priest "standing at the Lord's Table" then begins the Offertory with the customary sentences, the alms are presented, and the bread and wine placed on the Holy Table. The Intercession which follows may be in either the 1662 or the 1928 form, each now broken up into appropriate sections to allow a congregational response, "Hear us, we beseech thee". The Intercession in its twentieth-century form includes the commendation of the departed and thanksgiving for the saints. This ends the Antecommunion or Synaxis.

The Preparation for communion provides alternative and shorter forms of exhortation, confession, and absolution, followed by the Comfortable Words: and the Consecration begins with "The Lord be with you", Sursum Corda, Sanctus, and permitted *Benedictus qui venit*. Among the Proper Prefaces are some alternative or additional to those of 1662. The Prayer of Humble Access follows, and then the Prayer of Consecration. This may end as in 1662 or be followed by the Prayer of Oblation in shorter or longer form from the Canon of 1549. The shorter form reads: "Wherefore, O Lord and heavenly Father, we thy humble servants, having in remembrance the precious death and passion of thy dear Son, his mighty Resurrection and glorious Ascension, entirely desire thy fatherly goodness mercifully to accept this our sacrifice of praise and thanksgiving; most humbly beseeching thee to grant, that by the merits and death of thy Son Jesus Christ and through faith in his Blood, we and all thy whole Church may obtain remission of our sins, and all other benefits of his passion; through Jesus Christ our Lord, by whom, and with whom, in the unity of the Holy Ghost, all honour and glory be unto thee, O Father Almighty, world without end." The people answer Amen.

It will be noted that there is no Invocation of the Holy Spirit on the elements after the Words of Institution, which caused such trouble in 1928. From the standpoint of liturgy the new Consecration Prayer is, however, a great improvement on 1662, containing as it does an *anamnesis* or remembrance not only of the Passion but of the Resurrection and Ascension, though with no eschatological reference. It should also be noted that in the use of this prayer the bread may be broken either at the Words of Institution as in 1662, or the Lord's Prayer and fraction may follow the "Amen". Then, permissibly, come Pax and Agnus Dei and at the Communion either the 1549 or 1662 words of administration.

After communion come the Lord's Prayer, if not already said, alternative prayers of oblation (dependent upon what has already been said in the Canon) or of thanksgiving, the Gloria in Excelsis (which may be omitted), and the Blessing.

The basic structure of this rite remains that of 1662, with the significant addition of the Prayer of Oblation to the Consecration Prayer. The permissive addition of an Old Testament lesson, besides having ancient precedent, fulfils a real need, as does the permissive breaking up of the Prayer for the Church, giving it a litany structure: for experience has shown that prayers, if unduly long, require more concentration than this generation is able to give. But otherwise the defects of 1662 remain, and no new liturgical insights are embodied. The preparation of the elements is widely separated from their consecration. The Prayer of Humble Access still breaks the continuity which should run from "Let us give thanks" to the "Amen" of the Consecration Prayer. It thus remains a prayer and not a thanksgiving. Finally, no attempt has been made to authorize the use of the Psalter in the liturgy, as would seem desirable now that the Eucharist is the main, and for many the only, service of Sunday.

We turn now to the Order of Communion of 1967 (*Second Series*). Here the structure is clear. First the Antecommunion, consisting of an Introduction, the Ministry of the Word, and the Intercession; then the Communion, consisting of the Preparation of the People, the Preparation of the Bread and Wine, the Thanksgiving, the Breaking of the Bread, the Sharing of the Bread and Wine, and a Conclusion. The first part, the Antecommunion, corresponds to the ancient Synaxis, the church meeting open to all, centring round the ministry of the Word and ending with the prayers at which only the faithful were present. Gregory Dix called it "the Liturgy of the Spirit". The second part is the Eucharist proper, separable from the Synaxis, but in the normal worship of Sunday, anciently as now, combined with it. The use of the Introduction, apart from the greeting and invitation to prayer and the Collect of the Day, is optional; the Ten Commandments, our Lord's summary of the Law, and the Kyries are relegated to an appendix, and only the Collect for Purity and the Gloria in Excelsis are printed in the main text. Neither is an essential part of the service, and the Gloria can be sung as part of the conclusion of the whole rite, as in 1662. After the greeting and the Collect for the Day come the three lessons, Old Testament, Epistle, and Gospel, of which the Gospel and one other are compulsory, these being divided by Psalms or hymns.[1] The sermon, rightly, follows the Bible reading, and then the whole Ministry of the Word is summed up, at least on Sundays, by the Nicene Creed (with a slightly amended text).

The Intercession was, perhaps, the most dated part of the 1662 service—dated both in language and ideas. The 1967 prayer is wholly new, consisting, after the address to God, of four themes—prayer for the Church, the nations of the world, the suffering, and the departed— and a concluding petition. The prayer can be said as a whole (six short sentences) or each theme can be expanded, and made relevant to particular need, followed by "Lord, in thy mercy *Hear our prayer*". Alternatives (in an appendix) are a short litany and the Prayer for All Sorts and Conditions of Men, similarly divided into sections with a response "Lord, hear us. *Amen*". The intercession in the text is simple, flexible, and in every way to be preferred to 1662 or 1928, even as modified in First Series; but its form, as distinct from its content, is capable of improvement. If desired, this section of the service may close with a hymn and the collection, though not the presentation, of the alms.

The Communion begins with the Preparation of the People: an opening sentence, short Confession and Absolution, and the permissive use of the Comfortable Words and the Prayer of Humble Access. The shortening of the Confession with a less heavily weighted expression of guilt was expressly desired by the 1958 Lambeth Conference, and its wishes have been followed both here and in First Series. Some will undoubtedly feel that the brevity is excessive. Others

[1] The Liturgical Commission in 1969 has proposed the authorization of a new set of Collects and a new eucharistic lectionary, based on the work of the Joint Liturgical Group.

may be unhappy that the Prayer of Humble Access follows here and not, as in 1549, immediately before receiving communion, but at least its position is infinitely preferable to its disruption of the consecration in 1662 and First Series. Then follows the equivalent of the Kiss of Peace: "We are the Body of Christ. By one Spirit we are all baptized into one Body. Endeavour to keep the unity of the Spirit in the bond of peace. The peace of the Lord be always with you; *And with thy spirit*": a section which could perhaps be improved by the removal of the second hortatory sentence. The rubric then provides for a hymn, if desired, the collection of the alms, if that has not yet been done, and the preparation of the bread and wine. This makes possible an offertory procession where that is customary, but no form of words is suggested for an "offertory".

Then comes the Thanksgiving, called in a rubric the Prayer of Consecration. It should be noted that there is no separate Preface—the Thanksgiving is a unity—and the Proper Prefaces, to use our customary language, are inserted at the appropriate season into the opening section of this form of the ancient *eucharistia*, the thanksgiving to God through Christ over the bread and wine, for creation, incarnation, and redemption, for the calling of a people of God and the sending of the Spirit through the exalted Christ. To some it would appear that the Western "proper prefaces" are no longer needed. This section of the Thanksgiving culminates in the Sanctus. Perhaps it would have been too bold to reserve this for the final doxology; it now appears to be, what almost certainly it originally was, an interpolation into this section of the Thanksgiving. Then, with a prayer for the acceptance of the sacrifice of praise and that "these gifts of bread and wine may be unto us his Body and Blood", comes the central narrative of the Institution, the authority for all that we do, with simple manual acts as in 1549, but without the fraction, which, as in the narrative of the Upper Room, should follow the Thanksgiving. Finally come the Anamnesis, the prayer for true communion, and the doxology. In the Liturgical Commission's original draft, following ancient use, as for example in Hippolytus, this section began: "Wherefore, O Lord, having in remembrance his saving passion, his resurrection from the dead, and his glorious ascension into heaven, and looking for the coming of his kingdom, we offer unto thee this bread and this cup." In order to satisfy a body of Evangelical churchmen who felt unable to use the language of "offering" in this section of the Thanksgiving, the Convocations allowed "we give thanks to thee over" as an alternative to "we offer unto thee". The House of Laity, however, pleaded that there should be no alternatives at the heart of the rite and the form finally accepted for experimental use reads "with this bread and this cup we make the memorial of his saving passion" etc. Not all who opposed "we offer" would call themselves Evangelicals and not all Evangelicals would oppose it. But there can be little doubt that in its present form it does adequately express our obedience to our Lord's command to "do this in remembrance of me", or "do this for my memorial." And this is what matters. The Gloria makes a fine ending, but might be even finer if it led into the Sanctus.

The Thanksgiving can be followed by *Benedictus qui venit*. Then comes the Fraction, now rightly separated from the Institution narrative. It may be preceded by the quotation of 1 Corinthians 10.16–17, or accompanied by *Agnus Dei*. There follows the Lord's Prayer without the doxology as a preparation for communion, though many churchmen may well think it more appropriate in its 1662 position as the prayer of the Christian family renewed in Christ.

At the Communion, again following ancient precedent, the words of delivery of the bread and wine are "The Body of Christ" and "The Blood of Christ", to which the communicant makes the affirmation of faith "Amen"; but the Convocations have allowed as an alternative the present 1662 words.

This brings us to the Conclusion, which at present offers the alternatives of a prayer of thanksgiving, said by the Priest, which is a slight modification of 1662, or a prayer which can be said by all: "Almighty God, we offer thee our souls and bodies, to be a living sacrifice, through Jesus Christ our Lord. Send us out into the world in the power of thy Spirit, to live and work to thy praise and glory. Amen." It is a pity that this should be an alternative, for its emphasis on Christian life and witness, on mission, is otherwise absent from the service. The whole service ends "The Lord be with you; *And with thy spirit*. Go forth in peace; *Thanks be to God*" but with a rubric permitting Gloria in Excelsis, if it has not already been used before the Collect, to precede the dismissal. The Convocations permitted the addition of the customary Blessing or its use instead of the dismissal.

8

The Daily Services and Litany

MORNING and Evening Prayer are the Prayer Book version of the ancient Divine Office or Hour Services of the Church. They are "daily to be said and used throughout the year", that is to say in Church, and the obligation to say them either privately or openly is laid upon all priests and deacons. In 1552 preaching or study of divinity were allowed as reasons for their omission, but in 1662 this was altered to "sickness or some other urgent cause". The place in church where they are to be used is "the accustomed place". This, in 1549, was more specifically stated as "the quire", but in 1552 it was to be "used in such place . . . and the minister shall so turn him, as the people may best hear". A proposal was actually made that the chancels of churches should be destroyed so as to make all services congregational, and so as to abolish the medieval conception of the clergy as a priestly caste. This proposal was rejected, and the rubric states that "the chancels shall remain as they have done in times past". In Elizabeth's reign, however, several of the bishops ordered a reading pew to be set up in the nave—a magnificent example is still in use at Cumnor, near Oxford—and this became "the accustomed place". In some places this pew faced the congregation. The Canons of 1604 have the same object as the 1552 Prayer Book. The service is to be read "so as the people may be most edified". In parts of the country, however, the chancel screens which once supported the rood remained together with the choir stalls returned against the screen.

With this arrangement, the medieval one, the service must have been said facing East though the minister turned to the people when directed to do so by rubric.

The historical development of the two services which are identical in structure can be briefly stated. The 1549 core runs from the first Lord's Prayer to the third Collect, but with no Psalms as alternatives to the Canticles, and with the Creed among the suffrages. The penitential introduction was provided in 1552, and the prayers after the third Collect were transferred from the end of the Litany in 1662. The tendency of this development was to increase the importance of the daily services at the expense of Holy Communion. The additions of 1662 which included the occasional prayers really provide an alternative to the Litany, which was until then the Church's general intercession, but which the Puritans disliked. The anthem, also an addition at the Restoration, added to the musical attractiveness of the service which was increased by the use of hymns in the eighteenth century. The virtual inclusion within the services of the sermon was only the last stage of the provision of an alternative form of worship to that of the Sunday Holy Communion. Professor Ratcliff's comment is, "The Offices, as occasions of the ministry of the Word of God, became by a process natural within reformed circles, the central religious observances of English Church life."

The liturgical structure is set out in the opening exhortation which, however, has special reference to the 1552 additions to which it belongs. It therefore emphasizes confession of sin as man's duty at all times, but especially as preparatory to worship. That worship is then defined as thanksgiving and praise, the hearing of God's holy word and prayer; to which the Psalms and Canticles, the lessons, and the suffrages and collects correspond. The chief difference between this Prayer Book worship and that of the medieval Divine Office is the much larger place given to scripture and therefore to edification. Put another way, the earlier services were concerned solely with worship, and more particularly praise; the Prayer Book services have also as their concern the building up of the Church in its knowledge of Holy Scripture as the way not only of salvation but of Christian living. The relation in detail of Morning and Evening Prayers to the medieval services need not concern us. Morning Prayer is built up from Mattins, Lauds, and to a smaller extent Prime. The

83

medieval services began with the Lord's Prayer without the closing ascription, which did not appear even in the English books till 1662. The prayer, however, except for its closing "Deliver us from evil", was said privately, but in 1549 it was to be said aloud by the priest as in the Communion Service. The versicles and responses are from Mattins as are also the *Venite*, the *Te Deum*, and the lessons. *Benedictus* is from Lauds and also the Collect for peace. The Creed and the Lord's Prayer, both formerly said privately, the suffrages, and the Third Collect, are from Prime. In the same way Evening Prayer is built up from Vespers and Compline. Since both services have the same form they will not be further considered separately, but examined under the headings of their essential component parts.

The first of these consists of the Psalms and Canticles, the service of praise. The use of the Psalter, the Church's hymn-book from its earliest days, has already been briefly studied. The Prayer Book version is that of the Great Bible of 1539 and the translation is Coverdale's, made unfortunately from the Latin and German versions, and not from the Hebrew. It was retained in 1662 because of its familiarity and because it is easier for singing. The great beauty of its English rhythm has endeared it to Anglicans, but it sometimes strays far from the sense of the Hebrew. The scheme for its monthly cycle was, as we have seen, Cranmer's. He retained the very ancient use of the *Gloria* by which the Church claimed the psalter as her own and stamped it with the full revelation of God as a Trinity, but omitted the antiphons, which were in great measure an over-refinement and unsuitable to congregational worship. The 1928 Prayer Book has restored the antiphons of the *Venite*, here called invitatories, which relate the psalm to the season of the Church's year in which it is used. Proper psalms were restricted to four great feasts to which in 1662 were added the fasts of Ash Wednesday and Good Friday, but in the 1928 book they have been provided for every Sunday. This has the advantage of omitting from the Sunday service the psalms least suited to public worship, but has carried still further the tendency, begun with the proper lessons of 1559, to differentiate between the Sunday and week-day services, and to break up the scheme of orderly reading of Bible and Psalter which was Cranmer's guiding principle.

Side by side with the psalms we may consider the canticles and hymns. Canticles as distinct from psalms are scriptural hymns and are represented in the Prayer Book by the *Benedicite* from the Apocrypha and by the *Benedictus*, *Magnificat*, and *Nunc Dimittis* (which are the Canticles of Lauds, Vespers, and Compline) from the New Testament. Their use in worship is ancient, but they were disliked by the Puritans just because they derived from the old offices. Closely allied to them are the Christian hymns which are the natural fruit of Christian faith and joy. The New Testament in its later books has clear traces of hymn-making such as 1 Tim. 3.16, 1 Tim. 6.15–16, Rev. 15.3,4. The still later development is represented by the *Gloria in Excelsis*, first used at Mattins in the East and possibly also in the West; and, formed on the same model, the *Te Deum*, which according to Bishop Frere's suggestion replaced it when the *Gloria* was transferred to the Communion Service. St Ambrose was a great hymn writer of the early Church, and the "Athanasian Creed", which is a hymn about the Creed, is possibly his work. In the Middle Ages each office had its hymn, and it is simply owing to Cranmer's inability to write English verse (his translation of *Veni Creator* in the Ordinal shows how bad he was) that we are deprived of them. It was inevitable that when at the Evangelical Revival, and even earlier, Christian faith again expressed itself in hymns, these should find their way, even though unofficially, into the Prayer Book services. The provision of proper office hymns might secure the use of "objective" hymns, hymns of the faith, which would fit the scriptural character of Prayer Book worship and also relate it more closely to the Church's year. The only psalm appointed for use in 1549 as a canticle, and its use is very ancient, was the *Venite*. In 1552 alternatives were provided from the Psalter to the Gospel canticles— *Jubilate*, *Cantate Domino*, and *Deus Misereatur*. The real reason for this provision was the dislike of any similarity to the unreformed services, and it is doubtful whether the addition has in any way strengthened the service. *Benedicite* stands by itself. The 1928 book represents the shortened medieval form, but both in 1549 and 1552 it was printed in full, first as an alternative to *Te Deum* in Lent only and then without this restriction. This, surely, was a great mistake. The canticle, with its note of praise, does not fit Lent, and is far too long and monotonous for public worship. The suggestion of the Irish

Prayer Book, the hymn of Isaiah 26.1–8, is far better, or as has recently been suggested—Isaiah 12. A somewhat different criticism may be applied to the *Quicunque*, which was daily sung as a canticle at Prime and retained in 1549 after *Benedictus* for the six great feasts. Because of its teaching value and in days of theological unrest, it was prescribed for similar use on seven additional days in 1552, but at the Restoration it became an alternative to the Apostles' Creed. The 1928 Prayer Book has suggested its optional use, and produced a revised and improved translation, but it is more than doubtful whether it is suitable for worship except perhaps in a theological college. It might well be printed as a standard of orthodoxy, but the laity cannot understand it, and it is therefore a poor substitute for the directness and simplicity of the Apostles' Creed. The two great canticles, apart from those of Holy Scripture, are *Gloria in Excelsis* and *Te Deum*. The original *Te Deum* of the fourth century ended with the words, "Make them to be rewarded with thy saints in glory everlasting" (though owing to a misprint of the Latin from which it was translated we wrongly sing "numbered", *numerari*, for "rewarded", *munerari*). The verses which follow are suffrages, formerly variable, some of which anciently followed *Te Deum* and some *Gloria in Excelsis*. The daily use of this great model of Christian praise is one of the glories of the Anglican Prayer Book.

From the psalms and canticles we pass to the lessons. The problem of the lectionary is not solved even after three hundred years. Cranmer's scheme, with the addition of proper lessons for Sundays, stood till 1871, when the present "old" lectionary came into use. It is a compromise between Cranmer's scheme of continuous Bible reading based on the civil year and the quite different principle of following the Church's year. A further revision of 1922 produced an alternative table based entirely on the Church's year, and with considerably shorter lessons. In 1944 the Convocations approved two further schemes which after experimental use were replaced by yet a third in 1958. Underlying this history of revision are problems the full discussion of which must be reserved for the final chapter. The fundamental one is that only on Sunday is any considerable body of the laity present at the daily services. This makes special provision for Sunday a necessity, and breaks the course of weekly reading. Cranmer's principle of reading through the whole Bible in a year applies only to those who attend Mattins and Evensong daily, or use the Church's lectionary for their own Bible reading. For these, who in any case will hear or read, there is no particular merit in adhering strictly to the Biblical order of the Books, and this has generally been admitted in all recent revisions. For them, an additional set of Sunday lessons continuing the daily course might well be provided. But the real problem remains, the character of Sunday worship, the relation of Morning and Evening Prayer to Holy Communion, the provision in the lessons of that which will most truly edify, both from the Old Testament and the New. To these difficult questions we must come back.

The third section of Morning and Evening Prayer consists, liturgically, of the Suffrages and Prayers. This structure has, however, been disturbed, and for the better, in the course of Prayer Book revision. In 1549 the Creed, and Lord's Prayer, though said aloud by the priest, were placed as at Prime and Compline, among the Suffrages. This was changed in 1552, the Creed now said by minister and people, following the Canticle. This both gives greater dignity to the Lord's Prayer which follows, with its introductory Kyrie, and provides a fitting close to the ministry of the Word, the biblical revelation being summed up in the Creed, as at Holy Communion. The Creed, therefore, now belongs to the second section of the service, and its daily use by the whole congregation is one of the peculiar treasures of our English services. Founded on the most ancient of all the Creeds, the old Roman baptismal Creed, which goes back almost certainly to the second century, its simple narrative of the saving acts of God is especially suited to the needs of the ordinary Englishman, to whom it already belongs as the Creed of his baptism. Cranmer's second thoughts were in this case a great improvement.

The Suffrages and Prayers are introduced by the salutation: "The Lord be with you," and the response: "and with thy Spirit.' Minister and people are one as he prays in their name, or, as together, they share in suffrage and response. This salutation originally introduced the Collects, but now even more suitably stands at the head of all the prayers, including the Lord's Prayer, which thus is given the place of honour. The suffrages, which till 1662 were the only prayers for king, clergy, and people in the daily services, are taken not directly from the Breviary but from the Bidding of the Bedes, which normally took place after the offertory or before the sermon at Mass. This form of prayer in the common tongue, consisting of biddings, versicles, and responses, was popular in England and on the Continent. It survives in the Bidding Prayer before the sermon, now seldom found outside the older Universities but prescribed by the Canons of 1604; and here in Morning and Evening Prayer.[1] The response: "Because there is none other that fighteth for us, but only thou, O God," has been long felt to be inappropriate, and has been changed in most Prayer Books of the Anglican family, including the Proposed Book of 1928.

Then follow the Collects, beginning with the Collect for the Day. The word collect is from the Latin *collectio*, or in late Latin, *collecta*, which was used not only for prayer but of an assembly of people. In the Gregorian Sacramentary prayers in this form have the heading *ad collectam*, "for the assembly", and this probably refers to the ancient custom at Rome to go in procession to the church at which the Pope was celebrating. The *oratio ad collectam* was said when the procession was ready to set out, and again as the *oratio ad missam*, at the celebration of Mass. Thus the prayer for the day became the Collect. An alternative but less probable derivation is that the Collect was said at the end of a series of biddings, and thus collected or summed up private prayers. In any case, this form of prayer is very ancient, and the great majority of our Prayer Book collects, other than those for Saints' days, go back to the ancient Sacramentaries, Leonine, Gelasian, and Gregorian. The fact has already been noticed that the medieval mass contained beside the Collect for the Day the Secret and the Post-Communion, which were also Collects. The earliest Sacramentary, the Leonine, provides a fourth for every Mass, *oratio super populum*, so that there is an immense treasury of prayer of this type.

There are three main types of prayer, all of them to be found in our Prayer Book. The first is eucharistic and its English model is the Consecration Prayer with its Preface. A similar prayer is suitably provided in the 1928 baptismal office, and the prayers of the Ordinal

---

[1] The Bidding of the Bedes, or the Prone, has also been suggested as the source from which the Ten Commandments found their way into the service of Holy Communion.

immediately before the ordination, which throughout its history have been of this character, are marked off as such in 1928 by the provision of a preface. A similar prayer precedes the anointing of the king at his coronation. In general, eucharistic or consecratory prayer lies at the heart of every sacramental rite. The second type of prayer is Litany, with which we may include suffrage and bidding. Its essential character is that it is in the form of a dialogue. The third liturgical type is Collect, which is our present concern, though the later prayers of the Prayer Book tend to depart from the simplicity of the pure collect form.

The Collect is peculiar to the West. Eastern liturgical prayers are far longer and much more diffuse. In part the Collect owes its brevity, dignity, and conciseness to the genius of the Latin language in which it was first written. But the essential characteristic of the Collect is not brevity but unity of thought. Normally a collect consists of four closely related parts. First comes the invocation of God's name; and in the West prayer, and therefore the Collect, is normally addressed to God the Father. Then follows a clause which contains a divine attribute, "O God, whose never-failing providence ordereth all things in heaven and earth". Then comes the petition, or two if they are closely linked: "We humbly beseech thee to put away all hurtful things, and to give us those things which be profitable for us". Then, though not always, follows the purpose for which special grace is asked, and lastly the ending, usually a pleading of Christ's merit. The ancient form of ending was always constructed on the same model: "through Jesus Christ thy Son our Lord who liveth and reigneth with thee in the unity of the Holy Spirit, God for ever and ever". Unfortunately, following medieval custom, the Prayer Book collects were left without their endings till 1662, it being assumed that the simple rules were well known. The result is that they still are used in a shortened form only. But when the full form is there the result is a form of prayer of very great beauty and simplicity, which, more than any other characteristic of the Prayer Book, marks off the classical period of English liturgical construction from the modern age. Some seventy of our Prayer Book collects are translations of the ancient collects of the Sacramentaries. Some with their emphasis on human frailty reflect the conditions of the fifth century when the Pelagian heresy was fresh in the minds of men. Others of the same date were written at the time of the barbarian invasions when fear of enemies was widespread and prayer for deliverance natural and urgent. To realize this continuity of prayer from the days before Augustine came to England is to realize afresh the wealth of our Anglican heritage.

But besides the heritage of the centuries of Christendom, ours is also the heritage of the Golden Age of English prose, which is the sixteenth, not the seventeenth, century. The beauty of the Authorized Version of the Bible is due to the fact that fundamentally it is Tyndale's translation. The Revisers' own preface is by comparison turgid. But the great body of the Prayer Book is sixteenth century, and the English is that of one of the greatest masters of English prose, Cranmer. Nowhere is Cranmer's sense of form and command of words more plainly seen than in the collects. He does not translate but paraphrases. *Ecclesiam tuam illustra* becomes "cast thy bright beams of light upon thy Church"; *cui servire regnare est* becomes in English "whose service is perfect freedom". Sometimes, as in this latter instance, something is lost in the paraphrases, but Cranmer's achievement has never since been equalled. Some of the seventeenth-century prayers, as fresh compositions, are good; for example, Peter Gunning's "For all sorts and conditions of men" and Archbishop Laud's "for the High Court of Parliament", but the collects of this date tend to get longer and lose their form, as, for example, in the Collect for St Stephen's day by Cosin, which is a seventeenth-century expansion of 1549.

Beside the ancient collects there are just over thirty Reformation collects, mostly for saints' days, rewritten or freshly composed so as to avoid invocation of the saint. They are usually based on the Epistle and Gospel and contain more verbal quotation from Scripture than the older prayers, so that they tend to become clusters of texts. Even so, they have that all-important merit, proper rhythm. Compare, for example, Advent 2 and 3, both Cranmer's work of 1549. This then is our inheritance of liturgical prayer, and it is in the proper sense liturgical; that for which we pray is made possible by what God has shown himself to be. The very structure of the Collect bears witness to what, in the first chapter, we saw to be the essential character of liturgy. It is therefore all the more important that these liturgical prayers should be read with the gravity which is their due, for so only can they be truly prayed by the congregation.

The State Prayers belong, as we have seen, to the seventeenth century, but the final prayer is unique. It is found in the Eastern liturgy of St Chrysostom which Cranmer was studying. Presumably he took it from St Chrysostom, since he gives it the name of that saint. It belongs historically to a much later time than St Chrysostom himself, to whom it is ascribed, but it formed the perfect final prayer for Cranmer's litany of 1544 and was transferred with the State prayers to our daily services in 1662 and again is a perfect ending.

There is little that need be added about the provisions of First and Second Series. Each provides an enlarged series of opening sentences, some of them seasonal, and a shorter exhortation, confession, and absolution, but Second Series reverts to the order of 1549 by making the use of the penitential introduction optional. Each allows the shortening of the Venite; Second Series transposes Te Deum (without the suffrages) and Benedictus, provides a shortened version of the Benedicite, and ends the office at the Third Collect; but it may be followed by State Prayers, Occasional Prayers and Thanksgivings, or any other form of prayer authorized by the bishop. Among small improvements of detail may be noted that among the suffrages "Because there is none other than fighteth for us, but only thou, O God" is replaced by "For it is thou, Lord, only that makest us dwell in safety". These are very minor changes. The Commission, in the report which accompanied the text, says that no attempt has been made to answer the questions "Is it possible to provide an order of daily prayer which can in fact be used by clergy and laity alike?" and "What form should such an order take?" To answer these questions would require further consideration of the liturgical Psalter and lectionary. Even more revealing is their additional note in 1966: "We recognize that there is a strongly expressed desire for services alternative to Morning and Evening Prayer which will be different in structure, modern in language, and suitable to the needs of today."

The truth is that what Professor Ratcliff wrote soon after 1928, already quoted in this chapter, that "the Offices ... became the central religious observances of English Church life", has become a historical judgement which ceased to be true virtually from the time when it was written. The Sunday office has become a problem.

Attempts are being made to meet it,[1] but the root of the problem is with the very core of the office, the Psalter and the Lectionary. Convocation has authorized a new table of Sunday Psalms giving an average of sixteen verses at Mattins and twenty-four at Evensong. Lessons may be read in any of the versions, A.V., R.S.V., or N.E.B., but the difficulty has not been thereby overcome.

A quite separate problem is the relation of the weekday to the Sunday office. The former has virtually become a breviary for the clergy, the Psalms being said monthly, in course, and the lessons being long; and again there is something like a revolt against its use, especially among the younger clergy. Its reform did not fall within the terms of reference of the Liturgical Commission, but detailed suggestions have been published by the Joint Liturgical Group.[2] The Psalter is to be read on a quarterly instead of a monthly cycle; the long historical Psalms are shortened and the imprecatory Psalms omitted—omissions which the Church of Rome has also accepted. This provides approximately thirteen verses for each service. Lessons, two at Mattins and one at Evensong, average fifteen verses, the Old Testament being thus read in two years and the New Testament annually. Twelve canticles, some of them new to the English Prayer Book, provide for each service of the week, morning and evening, and thus relieve the services of the charge of monotony sometimes made. It remains to be seen whether these suggestions commend themselves to the Convocations; but if the Daily Office, involving as it does the regular use of the Psalter and the regular reading of the Bible, is to remain a part of the worshipping life of the Church of England, it is doubtful whether more can be done to meet the needs of this generation. A shortened form of the same office is provided for experimental use by the laity.

The Litany

The early history of the Litany form of prayer has already been considered. The English Litany dates from 1544, and its form is that of the Sarum Litany of the Saints with its characteristic section, the

[1] See John Wilkinson, *Family and Evangelistic Services*. 1967.
[2] *The Daily Office* by the Joint Liturgical Group. 1968.

invocation of the saints and the response *Ora pro nobis*, omitted. That Litany has an interesting history. It came to England at the end of the seventh century when the Pope was Sergius I, a Greek-speaking Pope from Antioch; and apparently he brought this Greek litany with him. From England it went to Ireland, where it is found in one of the most ancient liturgical books, the Stowe Missal. Later it was expanded from the earlier litany of the Latin West, the *Deprecatio* of Pope Gelasius I, a work of the fifth century preserved for us by Alcuin. Finally in its enriched form it went back to Rome, and was incorporated in the Roman services. This Sarum Rogationtide litany was the basis of Cranmer's work, as can be seen by an analysis of its structure. It consisted of:

1. The introductory Kyrie and invocation of the Trinity.

2. The invocation of the saints, with the response *Pray for us*.

3. The Deprecations, with the response *Deliver us, O Lord*.

4. The Obsecrations (e.g. By the Nativity) with the same response.

5. The Intercessions, with the response *We beseech thee, hear us*.

6. The invocation of Christ as the Lamb of God, followed by *O Christ, hear us*.

This Litany was used not only as a processional litany but as a stational litany, said kneeling before ordinations, at the blessing of the font and during Lent.

But beside the Sarum Litany Cranmer made use of two other important sources. One was the diaconal litany of the liturgy of St Chrysostom and the other Luther's litany of 1529 embodied in Hermann's *Consultation*, but probably already known to Cranmer before 1543. Out of these three strands and with some additions of his own Cranmer wove what has been called the most beautiful service in the English language. As it stands in our Prayer Book it is almost as it came from Cranmer's pen, except for the three invocations: Saint Mary, Mother of God; all Holy Angels and Archangels; all Holy Patriarchs, Prophets, and Apostles; which were all that remained of the long Sarum series in 1544. These were removed in 1549, and the deprecation, "from the tyranny of the Bishop of Rome and all his detestable enormities", disappeared at the beginning of Elizabeth's reign.

Cranmer, by combining the single deprecations and obsecrations of the Sarum service into groups of three, so working in his other sources, both shortened and enriched it. The intercessions are expanded, mainly from Luther, from whom comes also the Collect after the Lord's Prayer. The last petition is Cranmer's own work, and Bishop Frere's comment on it cannot be bettered: "The last suffrage has nothing corresponding to it in any other litany: it is a beautiful summary, expressing what we ought to feel at the conclusion of such petitions as have preceded: it is intended to supply any omission of a request, or of a confession, which ought to have been made: a prayer for repentance, forgiveness and the grace of amendment of life."[1] The final section, beginning "O Lord, arise, help us and deliver us" comes from the Sarum intercession in time of war, and is related to the condition of the country in 1544 when the English Litany first appeared. Liturgically it is interesting because it includes an example of the antiphons, which elsewhere in the Prayer Book have been omitted. "O God we have heard with our ears", etc., is a verse of Psalm 44. "O Lord arise" is its antiphon, and should both precede it and follow its *Gloria*. As the Book stands, possibly by mistake, the *Gloria* has become separated from its Psalm. Cranmer originally intended to produce a complete Processional which would have provided a series of endings suitable for different seasons. That he did not do so means that we have to use this war-time section for all occasions unless, following the 1928 book, it is agreed to omit it, for example when Holy Communion follows: or unless, like the Scottish Prayer Book, we produce new work comparable with the old.

The use of the Litany, preceding Ante-Communion, was ordered at first, in 1549, upon Wednesdays and Fridays: it was then sung. The notes at the end of the Book also imply that it would be used on Sundays. This was made explicit in 1552. In Elizabeth's reign the Sunday morning service became Morning Prayer, Litany, and Communion or Ante-Communion, and in 1662 the Litany was ordered to be sung or said after Morning Prayer, thus fixing its position. It thus

[1] Proctor and Frere, *A New History of the Book of Common Prayer*, p. 417.

forms the introductory Litany to Holy Communion characteristic of the early liturgies, and this same use of it is expressly ordered in the ordination services. There is, however, no hint in the Prayer Book that the Litany is to be sung in procession, and the rubric in Morning Prayer after the Collects implies that normally it was said rather than sung. The Proposed Book of 1928 restores its Rogationtide use.

Unfortunately the use of the Litany, especially on Sundays, is steadily declining, and this in a Church which possesses what is probably the most beautiful intercession in any language. The words of the Litany, said or sung sufficiently slowly to be grasped by the worshippers, cover the whole field of public prayer, and without this disciplined intercession, shared by all, the liturgy of the Church, her service of God and of man for God's sake, is incomplete. As we look back over the history of the service it becomes clear that its double origin, in connection with Holy Communion and as a penitential service on special occasions, is historically the cause of some, at least, of our present weakness. The Middle Ages taught the West to regard the Litany as a penitential procession the effectiveness of which was due to the invocation of the saints: hence its title. Otherwise it was never heard except by the devout few. The Prayer Book made its use regular, and restored the ancient connection with the Communion Service, but celebration of Holy Communion was infrequent until the Evangelical Revival and the Oxford Movement had done their work. The former produced an early celebration, the latter a High Mass divorced from Communion, but except in some cathedrals neither restored the Litany on Sunday, except as a permitted adjunct to Morning Prayer. The time has surely come to restore the Litany to its true position in Anglican worship whether in its present or in a shortened form. It will always be the service of the faithful who have really learned to pray, and its natural position is therefore its ancient one in the service of Holy Communion where it is already found at ordination.

The use of a litany—the Shortened Litany of the Scottish Prayer Book—has now been accepted as one form of the Intercession at the Communion, not however at the beginning of the Antecommunion, as in the Ordination rite, but at its end. (This, as we have seen, is where the Prayers of the Faithful were said in the early Church.) The Liturgical Commission has also provided both a slightly revised and a shortened form of the English Litany and also three short litanies, for the State, for the Church, and for the Common Good. The rubrics especially provide that particular intentions may be added to any petition, and this flexibility should make them useful wherever the litany form of prayer is acceptable.

9

The Occasional Offices

THE services of the Church cover the whole life of man. Holy
Communion and the Daily Services are regarded as the norm of his
adult life, and therefore have been considered in some detail in
previous chapters. The other services are occasional, and so may be
considered together, but they are nevertheless of varying importance.
Holy Baptism stands apart as one of the Sacraments of the Gospel
generally necessary for salvation. Closely associated with it since New
Testament times is Confirmation, to which the English Prayer Book
gave an added importance. In the Middle Ages penance, marriage,
ordination, and unction were also regarded as sacraments; and the
English Church, though refusing to regard them as sacraments of the
Gospel (Article XXV), preserved services which stand close to the
ancient rites of marriage and ordination, provided confession and
absolution for those who needed it, and for a time recognized a
modified rite of unction. To these must be added the Burial Office,
the Thanksgiving after childbirth, and the penitential devotion for
Ash Wednesday called the Commination. Of these eight rites the
Ordination Services stand separately in the Ordinal, and must be
separately considered. The others vary in importance and cannot all
be considered in detail.

With the Baptismal rites of the early Church, their continuance in
a compressed form throughout the Middle Ages, and the drastic
curtailment of their ceremonial at the Reformation, we are already

familiar: it is possible, therefore, to concentrate on the services themselves. The three services of the Prayer Book are all, however, similar in structure. The form of Adult Baptism was provided in 1662 when many children, having lived under the Commonwealth, had grown up unbaptized, and when the founding of the Colonies provided the Church with her first glimpse of missionary work. Its only significant difference from Infant Baptism is that the promises are made personally and the godparents appear only as witnesses.

The Baptismal Office of the 1549 book was a great advance upon the Sarum rite, the nature of which was obscured by the retention of the rites and ceremonies of the catechumenate. Even in the first Prayer Book the distinction between the admission to the catechumenate performed at the church door and the Baptismal Service at the font was still maintained. This, however, disappeared in 1552 when, as now, the whole service takes place at the font. Because its meaning includes the entry of the child into the Church of God the service follows the second lesson at Mattins or Evensong "when the most number of people may come together",[1] and this is still the Church's rule, though it is seldom observed.

The service provided by Cranmer in 1552 owes more than any other Prayer Book service to Hermann's *Consultation*. The opening exhortation, the first prayer (Luther's), the use of St Mark for the Gospel, the long exhortation, the prayer and the address to godparents which follow it, are all taken from this source, which accounts for the length and "wordiness" of the prayers when compared with normal Prayer Book use. With the Promises the service returns to older forms, but with a significant change. In the 1549 book, as in Sarum, the questions are addressed to the child, and the godparents gave what were regarded as the child's replies. In 1552 at Bucer's suggestion these questions were addressed to the godparents, though the last, "Wilt thou be baptized in this faith?", has, down to the present day, witnessed by an oversight to the earlier use. The 1928 book changes it to, "Dost thou in the name of this child ask for baptism?" Doctrinally this change is important. The Lutherans, while retaining infant baptism, justified its use on the ground of the vicarious faith of the godparents: hence Bucer's suggestion. This

[1] It is interesting that Bucer proposed to place baptism after the sermon at Communion because most people were then present.

doctrine appears to be supported by the Catechism, which down to 1662 answered the question, "Why then are infants baptized, when by reason of their tender age they cannot perform them?" (i.e. repentance and faith), with the reply, "Yes, they do perform them by their sureties." But 1662, though still addressing the godparents, makes it clear that they speak for the child ("Dost thou, in the name of this child?") and the Catechism was similarly altered. The doctrine of the Church is founded therefore upon the child's promise, and this led naturally to the renewal of vows in Confirmation, which is the distinctive feature of the Anglican service.

The custom of having godparents, or sponsors, is very ancient. In the third century there were two, one at admission to the catechumenate, one at the font, and though for a time only one was permitted, the addition of one at Confirmation gave the Sarum rule which says "two or three at most". In the English Church the Canons of 1603 require that godparents must have at least have received first communion, but the rule that parents cannot be godparents is no longer in force.

The Blessing of the Font was taken by Cranmer from a Gallican source,[1] and in 1549 consisted of a blessing, eight short petitions, and a collect. In 1552, in deference to Bucer, who objected to the blessing of inanimate objects as unscriptural, the rite was omitted, but in 1662 was restored in a shortened form with its present wording, "sanctify this water to the mystical washing away of sin".

Baptism in the name of the Trinity is immediately followed by the signing with the cross, the symbol of the life of discipleship begun, and by the reception of the child as a member of the Church, a beautiful gesture which is peculiar to our English service. As in Holy Communion, so here, the Lord's Prayer marks the climax of the service, and is followed by a prayer of thanksgiving composed in 1552. The final exhortation is common to all the Prayer Books, but the closing section on Confirmation appeared only as a rubric until the last revision.

In general therefore Baptism follows the traditional form, and its essential parts cannot be changed. Neither the Service of 1662 nor the very conservative revision of 1928 which modified the language of the prayers can be said, however, to meet the needs of the present

[1] The Mozarabic *Benedictio Fontis*.

generation. The language is still much too difficult, and indeed the underlying theology is not perspicuously clear even to theologians. The practice of indiscriminate Baptism has lowered a sacrament of the Gospel to a semi-magical rite, and the almost universal disregard of the opening rubrics has converted it into a private service. The case for revision is strong.

In the early Church the rite of confirmation followed Baptism immediately, but in the Middle Ages confirmation of infants was rare, though Queen Elizabeth was confirmed by Cranmer when three days old. Normally confirmation took place in childhood when the bishop was available. The Sarum service was brief. A prayer for the gift of the Holy Spirit and his sevenfold gifts preceded the anointing with chrism and the accompanying words, "I sign thee, N, with the sign of the Cross, confirm thee with the Chrism of Salvation, in the name of the Father and of the Son and of the Holy Ghost, Amen". With the prayer that the newly confirmed might "be fully perfected by the advent and indwelling of the Holy Ghost to be a Temple of His glory", and with a blessing the service closed. Communion followed "if his age demand it".

The first Prayer Book followed this model, but altered the formula of unction into prayer so as to refer not to the chrism but to Confirmation with inward unction of the Holy Spirit. Instead of the anointing, the bishop laid his hands upon the candidates with the words, "N, I sign thee with the sign of the Cross and lay my hand upon thee, in the name of the Father and of the Son and of the Holy Ghost, Amen". The Collect which now follows the Lord's Prayer, taken substantially from Hermann's *Consultation*, followed the laying on of hands and the service concluded with the Blessing. The service as printed included the Catechism, and its introduction suggests that the children confirmed would be examined in it by the bishop or his deputy.

The second Prayer Book removed the prayer for the inward unction of the Holy Ghost with its use of the word "confirm" and the signing with the cross. Instead, at the laying on of hands, the bishop said our present prayer, "Defend, O Lord, this thy child with thy heavenly grace". Otherwise the service remained unaltered.

In 1662 the Catechism, to which the section on the sacraments had been added in 1604, was separately printed. It had previously appeared under the general title "Confirmation, wherein is contained a Catechism for children". Confirmation, with its subtitle "Or laying on of hands upon those that are baptized and come to years of discretion", is now given a new Preface, and the old catechizing by the Bishop at his discretion is now represented by the one question in which the candidates are asked whether they "renew the solemn promise and vow that was made in your name at your baptism". The Lord's Prayer is inserted after the Confirmation, and the ancient collect which in 1549 stood at the end of the Communion service, "O Almighty Lord, and everlasting God", was most suitably inserted before the Blessing.

The developments in the Baptism and Confirmation services and in the Catechism since 1662 are sufficiently important to demand a detailed survey. The Catechism stands somewhat apart as its revision, long overdue, was not committed to the Liturgical Commission but to a special Archbishops' Commission appointed in 1958 at the request of the Convocations. The Revised Catechism was published in 1961 and includes additional teaching on the Church, the means of grace, the Bible, Christian duty, and the Christian hope, matters till then either inadequately dealt with or completely neglected in the Catechism. The report which introduced the Commission's work stressed the importance of using up-to-date language but rightly added: "It has not been possible, nor would it be desirable, to avoid using certain terms which belong to the technical language of theology. No one can enter into the heritage of Christian faith and worship without some understanding of these words, and in our view it is part of the responsibility of the catechist to explain them." Those who insistently and sometimes vehemently demand liturgy in equally up-to-date language should heed the *caveat*. The document will require some revision, as its authors recognize, in the light of the Baptism and Confirmation services published later, but it has won wide acceptance and will, no doubt, when revised, become fully authoritative.

The revisions of Baptism and Confirmation in 1928, now represented by First Series, are in the main conservative documents which retain the structure of the services. In Baptism the Augustinian language about original sin is softened and Old Testament references are removed. The promises made by the Godparents are slightly changed, e.g. "Dost thou in the name of this child profess the Christian Faith? *Answer*. I do", followed by the recitation of the Creed. The last question is "Dost thou in the name of this child ask for baptism?" The blessing of the water is now given the form of a consecration prayer. The service ends with a Blessing. Adult Baptism, similarly, is little changed. Confirmation was provided in 1928 with an alternative opening Preface, widely used, in the form of an address to the candidates which bases the whole rite on Acts 8, Peter and John's laying hands on the Samaritans baptized previously by Philip. The wisdom of so basing the Confirmation rite has been questioned by scholars, and the House of Laity took the decision not to sanction its continued use as a First Series experiment. Meanwhile the Liturgical Commission's first report (1958) on Baptism and Confirmation had been referred back by the Convocations. The main objections were to the Service for the Baptism of Infants, which was judged to be too complex in structure and not sufficiently simple in language. A second report was made in 1966, and the services annexed to it, belonging to the Second Series, have now been authorised for experimental use.

Second Series provides four services of Christian initiation which we may call (1) Adult Baptism and Confirmation; (2) Adult Baptism; (3) Infant Baptism; (4) Confirmation of those already baptized. Each may be combined with the Holy Communion, and each of the Baptism services may be inserted into Morning or Evening Prayer.

The first of these services, placed first because it retains the primitive unity of baptism and confirmation, opens with an Old Testament lesson, an Epistle (1 Cor. 12. 12–13) and has as its Gospel the account of our Lord's baptism from St Mark, with provision for hymns and specified Psalms between the lections. Then, after the Sermon, follows the Decision, in which the candidates affirm their allegiance to Christ and their rejection of all that is evil. Then comes the Blessing of the Water, setting out the meaning of baptism as baptism into Christ's death and newness of life in the power of the resurrection, dependent on Christ's death and the sending of his Spirit. The affirmation of faith is made immediately before baptism: "Do you believe and trust in God the Father? in his Son Jesus Christ? in his Holy Spirit?" Each answer is given in the form "I believe and trust in Him". Then, following the baptism itself, the signing with the Cross and the permissive gift of a lighted candle, the significance of each ceremony being explained in words said by the congregation; and the newly baptized may be welcomed by the congregation since "God has received you by Baptism into his Church". Then, at once, the Bishop ministers Confirmation. Stretching out his hand over the candidate, he says: "Almighty and everlasting God, who in baptism hast caused thy servants to be born again by water and the Spirit and hast given unto them forgiveness of all their sins: Send forth upon them thy Holy Spirit . . ." and there follows the prayer for the sevenfold gifts of the Spirit. On each candidate he lays his hands, saying: "Confirm, O Lord, thy servant [N.] with thy Holy Spirit." The People then say with the Bishop the 1662 Confirmation Prayer, "Defend, O Lord", and Communion follows, beginning with the Preparation of the Bread and Wine.

The Baptism of Adults follows this same order but adds the Lord's Prayer, a thanksgiving, and a prayer "that, fulfilled by thy Spirit, they may live and grow in thy service and attain thy promises"; the service closing with the Grace.

Similarly the Confirmation of those previously baptized follows precisely the same order previously described. It is prefaced by the Decision and the Profession of Faith, which precede the Baptism in the combined service. If there is no Communion, then, as in 1662, the Lord's Prayer, a Collect, and the Blessing follow.

The Liturgical Commission's report on its Confirmation service is worth quoting.

Three views have been current in the Church [about the relation between baptism and confirmation].

The first view is: Baptism in water is the sacramental means by which the Spirit is given to Christians. Confirmation is the occasion on which Christians renew the acts of repentance and faith which were made in their name, or which they themselves made at their baptism. They do this in the presence of the bishop, who solemnly blesses them; and this blessing may be regarded as an occasion of grace.

The second view is: Baptism in water is the sacramental means by which the Spirit is given to Christians. Confirmation is a second sacramental act, consisting of prayer for the coming of the Spirit, with laying on of hands upon those upon whom the Spirit is asked to come. It effects a further work of the Spirit, to assist them to grow in the Christian life, and to strengthen them against temptation.

The third view is: Baptism in water and prayer with the laying on of hands together constitute the sacramental means by which the Spirit is given to Christians. If the two sacramental acts are distinguished in thought or separated in practice, the Spirit is thought to come in baptism to effect cleansing from sin and new birth, and in confirmation to complete the divine indwelling.

We have tried to draft these services in such a way as neither to exclude not to assert exclusively any one of these views. Thus, no use has been made of the *scripture passages* in Acts 8. 14–17 (Peter and John at Samaria) and 19. 1–7 (Paul at Ephesus) since this might be thought to identify confirmation with these events. But the phrase "after the example of thy holy apostles", which has appeared in every English Prayer Book since 1549, has been retained.

The service of Infant Baptism differs widely from both 1662 and the First Series and therefore requires a full description. It has a Preface stating that infants are baptized on the understanding that they will receive a Christian upbringing, and requiring the priest to ask the parents and sponsors whether by teaching and example they will help the child to be regular in public worship and private prayer and encourage him to come to Confirmation and Communion. Then, instead of the three lessons and sermon of the Adult service come four short passages about baptism in the New Testament, beginning with our Lord's; these lead into a thanksgiving by all for their own baptism and a prayer for those to be baptized, said by all. The Decision follows, as in the Adult service, the questions being asked of both sponsors and parents and answered by them. The water is blessed, and the Baptism follows. The parents and sponsors make the affirmations of faith, having first been told: "You have brought these children to Baptism. You stand in the presence of God and his Church. You must now make the Christian profession in which they are to be baptized, and in which you will bring them up." The post-baptismal ceremonies are those of the Adult service, a sponsor receiving the candle. After the Lord's Prayer there is a thanksgiving that those baptized have been born again and a prayer that they may grow in the faith in which they have been baptized and themselves profess it when they come to be confirmed, and that all things belonging to the Spirit may live and grow in them. After a blessing on the parents and a prayer for wisdom and love in their home, the service closes with the Grace. It will be noted that no questions are asked of the child and no promises made by godparents in the name of the child. The report introducing the service says:

In this Service, where the profession is made by the parents and sponsors, the question arises, "Whose renunciation and faith is professed?" Is it the present renunciation and faith of the parents and sponsors, or the future renunciation and faith of the child? We have tried to make the words of the service cover both views. The present renunciation and faith of the parents and sponors is professed in their rejection of all that is evil and their belief and trust in God. The future renunciation and faith of the child is affirmed by his baptism in this profession, in which it is the duty of the parents and sponsors to bring him up. In this way we have tried to retain the view expressed in 1662, that the child promises "by his sureties" that he will renounce and believe, while placing responsibility for the implementation of this promise upon the shoulders of those who made it on the child's behalf.

Two other sacramental rites of the Middle Ages were still retained in a modified form in 1549, Confession and Absolution (the "sacrament of penance"), and Unction: both were to be found in the Order for the Visitation of the Sick. There the sick person is exhorted to forgiveness of injuries, reconciliation, restitution, and the setting of his affairs in order, after which the rubric directs that "the sick person shall make a special confession, if he feel his conscience troubled with any weighty matter. After which confession the priest shall absolve him after this form: and the same form of absolution shall be used in all private confessions." The last part of this rubric referring to private confessions was removed in 1552, but the first part was strengthened in 1662 where the sick person "shall be moved to make a special confession". Furthermore the exhortation in the Communion service, though it specifies no form of absolution, still suggests private confession to those who need it. A fair statement of the Anglican position is Moberly's. "The Reformers desired to regulate auricular confession to the abnormal, to the class of medicine rather than normal Christian life." Hooker (Eccles. Pol. Book 6, cap. 2) puts it more strongly: "We labour to instruct men in such manner that every wounded soul may learn how to heal itself; they, on the contrary, make all spiritual sores seem incurable unless the priest have a hand in them." There is, indeed, a fundamental difference between the medieval (and Roman) and the Anglican *doctrine* of penance. In the medieval system the sacrament of penance is the divinely appointed way of dealing with post-baptismal sin, and is therefore obligatory, and in cases of mortal sin, necessary. The Anglican Church requires private confession of no man, but provides for it in cases of need and commits to her priests the authority from her Lord to absolve those who are truly penitent and desire absolution. There is a great gulf here, the nature of which is clear in the writings of the Reformers. "With us", says Hooker again, "the remission of sins is a thing which is ascribed unto God as proceeding from Himself, and following immediately on true repentance, but that which we attribute to the virtue of repentance they impute to the sacrament of repentance, and having made repentance a sacrament, and thinking of sacraments as they do, they are found to make the ministry of the priest and their absolution the cause of that which God worketh." It only remains to be noticed that the form of absolution "I absolve thee" dates only from the twelfth century, the more ancient form being the prayer which immediately follows.

The other sacramental rite also modified at the Reformation is the anointing with oil. The scriptural basis for this is St James 5.14, "Is any sick among you? Let him call for the elders of the church; and let them pray over him, anointing him with oil in the name of the Lord: and the prayer of faith shall save the sick: and the Lord shall raise him up, and if he have committed sins, they shall be forgiven him." This in the Middle Ages had become the sacrament of extreme unction conferred only when there was no hope of recovery. The Prayer Book of 1549 restored the scriptural emphasis using anointing for recovery of health both of body and soul. The rite was very simple. It followed the careful preparation of the Visitation which preceded it including confession and absolution, and consisted of anointing upon the forehead or breast only with the sign of the cross; and a prayer similar to that of Confirmation, praying for the inward anointing of the soul with the Holy Ghost, restoration of health, "release of all thy pains, troubles and diseases, both in body and mind", forgiveness for the past and spiritual power for the future. Psalm 13 follows. This beautiful and entirely scriptural service was omitted in 1552 and has never been restored, though the 1928 Book provides that the minister shall pray, "laying his hands upon the sick person if desired".

To these rites of the Visitation of the Sick we can add the Communion of the Sick. In the Middle Ages this was always Communion from the Reserved Sacrament. The practice of continuous reservation was already discarded in 1549, but the ancient practice of the early Church was restored, whereby the consecrated elements were taken straight from the church to the sick. Justin Martyr mentions that in the second century the deacons performed this office; Eusebius says a boy used to carry the elements, and Jerome mentions a glass and a wicker basket. In the Middle Ages the Host was carried with a lighted candle and the ringing of a bell. In the first Prayer Book the presence of others beside the sick person was desired, but not insisted upon, and the short service in the sick room included confession, absolution, the Comfortable Words, and, after Communion, the Prayer of Thanksgiving. If there was no open Communion on the given day a special celebration at the house takes the place of what has been called "extended Communion". In 1552 even this modified form of reservation was abandoned by omitting the rubrics concerning it, leaving only those which governed the ministry of the Holy Communion. No attempt to restore it was made in 1662 when the rubric commanding the reverent consumption of what remains of the consecrated bread and wine was inserted; and the attempt to do so in 1928 was a major cause of the controversy which led to the rejection of the Book by Parliament.

The last of the rites "commonly called sacraments" is the Solemnization of Holy Matrimony. This service lies nearest to the medieval rite of any in the Prayer Book, and only needs brief comment. In the early Church no ecclesiastical law obliged Christians to seek a blessing on their marriage. No service goes back to the New Testament, and when we find services they bear no trace of Jewish ancestry. The service of the Prayer Book is, indeed, essentially the Roman form of Patrician marriage celebrated with the Church as witness and with the Church's blessing added. Put another way, it is the pagan rite of betrothal transferred to the Church; the Eucharist, including a nuptial blessing, taking the place of the ancient pagan sacrifice. The ceremony of the ring (until 1547 placed on the fourth finger of the right hand) and the joining of hands are both pre-Christian. The placing of the ring on the Book, however, is an acknowledgment that all our worldly goods belong to God; and the "giving away" of the bride was originally a giving to God who bestowed her on her husband as God gave Eve to Adam. So, in the York Manual, the sentence reads: "Who gives me this wife?"

the priest being God's minister. The pronouncement that the pair, after the blessing, are man and wife is taken from Hermann's *Consultation*.

Until 1662 the Communion Service, which in the early Church was the confirmation or seal of the marriage, followed immediately. This is implied in the 1549 book, and made explicit in 1552. "Then shall begin the communion." In the Middle Ages the practice of receiving Communion at a wedding had died out, though the Mass, of course, remained. The Prayer Book insisted upon the newly married persons receiving Communion the same day as their marriage. The exhortation, now seldom read, at the end of the Service, is only a permitted substitute for the sermon of the Holy Communion Service. In 1662 the Caroline Divines had to be content with the second best, "It is convenient that the persons newly married should receive the Holy Communion at the time of their marriage, or at the first opportunity after their marriage."

Apart from the minor offices which will be left without comment, only the service for the Burial of the Dead now remains. The medieval office of *Placebo*, *Dirige*, and *Requiem* we have already examined. The office of 1549 was a drastic revision but consisted of the same essential parts—the procession, the office, the burial, and the Communion—in their Reformation form. The procession is not from the house but from the church stile—that is the lych gate (*lich* being Anglo-Saxon for corpse), so named because the bearers of the dead might rest there and deposit their burden. The procession went straight to the grave, the priest singing the Sentences. At the grave-side, while the grave is made ready, the Sentences continue as in the present service, the first being taken from Sarum, the rest from a Lenten antiphon to *Nunc Dimittis* composed by Notker, a monk of St Gall, in the ninth century. Luther turned it into a hymn, and Coverdale into English, so suggesting its use here. The priest casts earth on the body with its committal to the earth in hope of the resurrection and the commendation of the soul to God. The office, consisting of Psalms, lesson, suffrages, and one prayer follows but may precede the burial. Finally comes Communion with 1 Thessalonians 4.13–18 for the Epistle and part of St John 6.37–40 as the Gospel.

This service, itself far more beautiful and much less gloomy than the medieval rite, was mutilated, the only possible word, in 1552. All that remained was the opening sentences, the committal without commendation, the lesson, apparently to be read at the graveside, the lesser Litany, Lord's Prayer, and two following prayers, the second still marked as the Collect, though the Communion to which it belonged was removed. There is, in fact, no reference to a service in church. It looks as though the revision was hastily done and consisted in the removal of all prayers for the dead.

In 1662 order was restored. The office, as in 1549, can be said either before or after burial. To it the Psalms and lesson are restored, but not the suffrages. The rest of the service takes place at the graveside, and follows 1552, with the addition of the grace.

When the reformed service is compared with the medieval, apart from differences of structure, a marked difference of emphasis is at once apparent.[1] The whole medieval emphasis is upon judgment— *dies irae*. In the Prayer Book the emphasis is upon the power of Christ's resurrection. The change is due to the abandonment of the doctrine of Purgatory. The medieval Catholic of his charity prayed for all the dead except the saints, for Purgatory was the common expectation of all men. The Reformers, finding no scriptural warrant for such prayers, removed them from the public worship of the Church, and charitably left their dead to the mercy of Christ. Unfortunately, but understandably, they abolished the Communion also, for inevitably it would have been interpreted in the sixteenth century as a Requiem. But in no other way can the Communion of Saints be so truly realized, and rightly the 1928 book restores it. What is much less clear is whether its other suggestions imply a reformed or a medieval view: they appear to be nearer the latter. In any case its rubrics are far too complicated and almost any number of different services can be constructed by means of them. There is still room for revision.

[1] Lowther Clarke, *Liturgy and Worship*, p. 623.

10
The Ordinal

THE ministry of the Church as we find it, for example, in the letters of Ignatius at the beginning of the second century, consists of a threefold order of bishops, presbyters, and deacons. The differentiation between bishop and presbyter must then have been comparatively recent, for it is not made in the New Testament, and is apparently unknown to Clement of Rome in A.D. 96. There is still no agreement among scholars as to how the change came about, for the evidence is far too scanty. In any case, the gap left by the death of the Apostles and of apostolic delegates like Timothy and Titus had to be filled, not indeed by a permanent apostolate, for the apostle was essentially a personal witness to Christ, but by a differentiation between the presiding elder or bishop and his colleagues. The Preface to the English Ordinal is, therefore, not far wrong when it says that "it is evident unto all men, diligently reading holy scripture, and ancient authors, that from the Apostles' time there hath been these orders of ministers in Christ's Church: Bishops, Priests and Deacons"; priest being the English form of presbyter. It might have added that the early Church possessed also an order of deaconesses from the time of the Apostles, and maintained it till the sixth century, that is so long as the adult baptism of women was the rule. They helped at the administration of baptism and at the *Agapé*, or love-feast, but not at the Eucharist.

To the Holy Orders minor orders were soon added. In the second century we meet with sub-deacons and acolytes, lectors at its close, and slightly later exorcists and doorkeepers. A list of the Roman clergy given in a letter of Pope Cornelius in 251 includes the bishop, forty-six priests, seven deacons, seven sub-deacons, forty-two acolytes, and fifty-two lectors, exorcists, and doorkeepers, but only those in Holy Orders were ordained, and candidates for the ministry began as lectors, or readers.

Ordination from the time of the New Testament was by laying on of hands and prayer, cf. Acts 6.6, 1 Timothy 4.14, 2 Timothy 1.6, and the narrative of the appointment of the seven "deacons" of Acts 6 suggests that election or approval by the Church necessarily preceded ordination. The ceremony of "laying on of hands" goes back to the appointment of Joshua as the successor of Moses in Numbers 27.15–23. Joshua[1] is a man in whom is the spirit: laying on of hands is the outward sign of the sharing of Moses' ministry. The elders of the Jewish synagogues were ordained with laying on of hands, the Old Testament precedent being the divine ordination of the original seventy recorded in Numbers 11.16–25, a passage quoted in later Christian Ordinals. Laying on of hands expresses identification, and separation for a divinely appointed work, rather than transference. This is clear from the parallel Old Testament ritual in which the sinner lays his hand upon the sacrificial victim with which he identifies himself, and which he separates for the divinely appointed rite of sacrifice. In the New Testament this comes out clearly in Acts 13.1 where the Church at Antioch separates Barnabas and Saul for their God-appointed work, and identifies itself with the Apostles in their mission. The other essential element in ordination to the ministry is the operation of the Spirit of God. This is clear even in the Old Testament passages already quoted but it is clearer still in the New Testament. It is the meaning of St John 20.22–23 and of 1 Corinthians 12.4ff. The one Lord calls, endows, and uses his ministerial servants by his Spirit; but through men already so called, endowed, and used. So the first Christian writer outside the New Testament, Clement of Rome, speaks of the Apostles as "going forth with full conviction from the Holy Spirit", "proving by the Spirit" their converts, and so appointing them bishops and deacons. On the basis of ordination by laying on of hands and prayer thus understood the ordination services of the Church are built.

The earliest which we possess is the *Apostolic Tradition* of Hippolytus early in the third century. In this there is an interesting

[1] Cf. Num. 8.10–13 : The Ordination of the Levites.

connection between the ordination of bishop and presbyter. "When a presbyter is ordained let the bishop lay his hand on his head, the presbyters also touching it together, and let him speak according to what has been said before, just as we have said before over the bishop." When, however, a deacon is ordained the bishop alone is to lay on his hand for the deacon is the bishop's minister (or assistant). The prayer at the ordination of a presbyter may be quoted as the earliest we possess. "God and Father of our Lord Jesus Christ, look down on this thy servant and impart the Spirit of Grace and counsel of the presbyterate, that in a pure heart he may aid and govern thy people, as thou didst look down upon the people of thy choice and didst order Moses to choose presbyters, whom thou didst fill with thy Spirit, which thou gavest to thy servant: and now, O Lord, vouchsafe to preserve in us unfailingly the Spirit of thy grace, and make us worthy that, believing in thee, we may minister in simplicity of heart, praising thee, through thy Child Christ Jesus, through whom be glory and power to thee, Father and Son, with the Holy Spirit, in the Holy Church, both now and evermore. Amen." It is to be noted that no sacrificial functions are mentioned, though the bishop's are said to include those of propitiation and of offering the gifts of the Holy Church.

As the centuries pass, however, the sacrificial doctrine of the Eucharist as the offering of the Body and Blood of Christ, increasingly emphasized the sacerdotal view of the ministry the growth of which, as Lightfoot remarked, is one of the most striking and important phenomena in the history of the Church. Whereas in the New Testament the word priest (*hiereus*) is nowhere used of the Christian ministers the equivalent Latin *sacerdos* came to be his normal designation. In Hadrian's Sacramentary, representing the developed Roman rite, the Old Testament reference is not only to the prophetic spirit given to the elders but also to the Aaronic priesthood, and the wording of the whole prayer is sacerdotal. It remains true, however, that for all these orders the form was still primitive and simple, the laying on of hands with prayer. The setting of the service was, as in the days of Hippolytus, the Holy Communion. The candidates were presented to the Church, and, except at Rome, were acclaimed as worthy of ordination. They were presented to the bishop by the archdeacon; prayers and the Litany were said, and the laying on of hands followed with a double consecratory prayer. The only major difference in the consecration of a bishop was that everywhere except at Rome the open Book of the Gospels was held over the head of the candidate to symbolize ordination by our Lord himself.

The minor orders were not conferred by laying on of hands, but the candidates were given a blessing and a symbol of their office. This ritual was most developed in Gaul where the doorkeepers are given a key, lectors a book of lessons, exorcists a book of exorcisms, acolytes a candle and cruet for wine, subdeacons a paten and chalice by the bishop and a basin, ewer, and napkin by the archdeacon. In course of time it was natural that a similar "tradition of the instruments" should develop for Holy Orders, and in the ninth century we find the deacon being given the Book of the Gospels with the charge to read the gospel; the priest chalice and paten, with wine and bread prepared, with the charge to offer the holy sacrifice; and the bishop staff and ring, with the charge to maintain discipline and be sound in the faith. A formula was also added to the more ancient ceremonies of vesting.

In an earlier chapter we have seen that in the West the Roman and Gallican rites interacted with the final production of a modified Roman rite. In the ordination services both rites survived, with the result that in the combined rite almost everything was done or said twice. There were actually a double laying on of hands, one Gallican and one Roman, two bidding prayers, and two consecratory or ordination prayers, the Gallican and the Roman; but the services were so constructed that the two similar prayers or ceremonies never followed one another directly. The result was a most confused service, as may be seen from a brief inspection of the ordination of deacons and priests. Here after presentation and enquiry we have:

> Litany with Special Clauses (Roman).
> Instruction of the Candidates.
> Imposition of Hands in Silence (Gallican).
> Bidding Prayer and Collect (Roman).
> Consecratory Prayer (Roman).
> Vesting with Stole: Giving of the Book of the Gospels.
> Bidding Prayer (Gallican).
> Consecratory Prayer (Gallican).
> Vesting in Dalmatic.

The Gospel

Instruction of Priests.

Imposition of Hands by Bishop and Priests in Silence (Gallican).

Bidding Prayer and Collect (Roman).

Consecratory Prayer (Roman).

Vesting with Stole and Chasuble.

Bidding Prayer (Gallican).

Consecratory Prayer (Gallican).

Veni Creator.

Blessing and Anointing of Hands (Gallican).

Tradition of the Instruments.

The Communion Service to the Communion

Imposition of Hands with formula "Receive the Holy Spirit" (Roman).

Blessing.

Communion Service to the end.

It was this muddled service which made it so difficult in the Middle Ages to say when or with what form a priest was ordained, for in very truth he was ordained twice. Pope Eugenius IV even told the Armenians in 1439 that the essential rite of the service, its form and matter, consisted of the delivery of the instruments with the accompanying formula: which if true would mean that no priest was ordained for nearly the first thousand years of the Church's life! This, then, was Cranmer's liturgical inheritance, and to his work we must now come.

The principle of reform, as the Preface to the Ordinal shows, was to continue the threefold ministry by the New Testament method of ordination by public laying on of hands and prayer. This, as Duchesne points out, is the only essential of valid ordination. The main lines of the old service, with its doublets removed, were retained, ordination being set in the context of the Holy Communion with the Litany in its ancient place. The tradition of the instruments was retained in a modified form. In the first ordinal of 1550 the bishop was given his pastoral staff, the priest a Bible in one hand and the chalice in the other, the New Testament to the deacon. From 1552 onwards the New Testament was given to deacons and the Bible to priests and bishops. Even the formula "Receive the Holy Spirit", a comparatively late medieval addition, was retained in what is liturgically a conservative revision. The English form, though based on far less knowledge of early ordination services than we now possess, did succeed in emphasizing the essential rite of the New Testament and the early Church. Its one mistake, as we now realize, is that by its use of the formula "receive the Holy Spirit" (no doubt because it was scriptural) the emphasis is diverted from the prayer which precedes it; and it is the language of the prayer which is all important.

There are, however, significant changes in the Prayer Book services. The most important of these is the redefinition of the function of the priest implied both by the change in the instruments and by the address to those about to be ordained. All sacerdotal language is removed: the Anglican priest is a presbyter not a sacrificing priest. All the emphasis in the solemn address falls on the pastoral and prophetic aspects of the work of the ministry. The space given to this address, itself a new element in the service, is due to the anxiety of the Reformers to make clear the sense in which they understood the function of the priesthood. But their primary intention is made clear by the language of the ordination prayer itself. The bishop prays that those to be ordained to the priesthood may be endued with grace for "the same office and ministry appointed for the salvation of mankind" which our Lord instituted by sending into the world his Apostles, Prophets, Evangelists, Doctors, and Pastors. The Church of England ordains to the ministry of the Church of God, and goes back to the New Testament for the understanding of its nature. When Roman Catholic writers claim, as some have done, that the "intention" of the Church of England changed at the Reformation, that from 1550 she did not intend to make a priest in the sense of one whose chief function is "offering the sacrifice of the Mass for the living and the dead", the claim should be candidly admitted. But when the deduction is drawn that the rite is therefore invalid it can be strenuously resisted. The Anglican intention is clear: it is the Roman which is debased.

The second main change is the introduction of a detailed examination and instruction of the candidates for the diaconate and priesthood: the earlier rites having included these only for the bishop. This carries out the requirements of the Preface to the Ordinal that candidates must be "first called, tried, examined, and known to have such qualities as are requisite", with the further recognition that the Church, represented by the congregation at the service, has the right to be satisfied of these things if it is to concur in all that is done. It should further be noticed that the Ordinal explicitly recognizes that an essential of true vocation is God's call to ministry. "Do you trust that you are inwardly moved by the Holy Ghost to take upon you this Office and ministration" is the first question asked of the man about to be made deacon.

Of the Ordination Services, as of the Prayer Book, it is true that our present services are substantially those of 1552. Only minor changes were made in 1662, and these insist on episcopal ordinations as a condition of ministry in the Anglican Church, strengthen the wording so as carefully to define the office to which the ordinand is admitted, and make it clear that the distinction between bishop and priest is a real one. The Puritans claimed that the use of the word pastor in describing the work of the presbyters gave him the same office as the bishop. The word was therefore removed both here and in the Litany, thus defining more carefully the difference between Episcopal and Presbyterian or Congregationalist conceptions of Church order.

In conclusion it can be said with truth that here is a service both Catholic and Reformed which expresses the mind of the Church, is firmly scriptural, and both preserves and enriches the liturgical inheritance of the English Church.

To this account of the English Ordinal must now be added an equally brief analysis of the draft Ordinal of 1968, prepared by a joint Anglican–Methodist committee with the best liturgical advice in the course of negotiations for the reunion of the Churches. This is, indeed, an excellent document, which has the particular merit of making clear that it is the content of the ordination prayer which is of supreme importance. Whether the ordination be of deacon, presbyter, or bishop, the laying on of hands takes place at the heart of this prayer. All ordinations are to take place in the course of the Eucharist after the Ministry of the Word. The pattern is basically that of the Anglican Ordinal, and is the same for all three orders of ministry, namely Presentation to the Bishop, or Presiding Bishop, followed by the assent of the Church, the Examination, the Supplication or prayer of the congregation, summed up in a Collect and followed by *Veni Creator*. Then comes the Ordination, the words used at the laying on of hands being always "Send down thy Holy Spirit upon thy servant N. for the office of (Deacon, Presbyter, or Bishop and Chief Pastor) in thy Church." Ordination is followed by the giving of the Bible to the newly ordained. The new presbyters or bishops then concelebrate with the Bishop by joining with him in reciting the Thanksgiving. At the ordination of a presbyter, presbyters, not less than three in number, lay on hands with the Bishop, and at the ordination of a bishop, not less than three bishops lay on hands.

The portion of the Ordination Prayer defining the ministry to which a man is ordained is so important doctrinally that it must be quoted. For the priesthood:

Pour forth thy grace upon these thy servants, we beseech thee, O Lord, that within the royal priesthood of thy People they may faithfully fulfil this their priestly ministry. Grant that as true pastors they may watch over the sheep committed to their care . . . Strengthen them to proclaim effectually the Gospel of thy salvation, and to declare to the penitent the absolution and remission of their sins. Make them worthy to offer with all thy People spiritual sacrifices acceptable in thy sight, and to minister the sacraments of thy New Covenant . . . Make them to be apt and profitable fellow-workers with their brethren in the Ministry and with thy chief pastors, the Bishops. . . ."

and for the episcopate:

"Endue him, we pray thee, as thou didst endue thine Apostles, with the fullness of thy grace, that he may be worthy, as a true shepherd, to feed and govern thy flock; to offer with all thy people spiritual sacrifices acceptable in thy sight; to preside at the Sacrament of the Body and Blood of thy dear Son: and to promote unity and love within thy Church. . . .

The functions of the orders of ministry are still further defined in the Examination. Thus, a bishop is called to be

a Chief Minister and Chief Pastor and, with other Bishops, to be a guardian of the faith, the unity, and the discipline which are common to the whole Church, and an overseer of her mission throughout the world . . . to govern after the example of the Apostles of the Lord. . . . to lead and guide the Presbyters and Deacons under his care and to be faithful in ordaining and sending new ministers . . . and lead [his people] in the offering of spiritual sacrifice and prayer.

Some criticism has been made of the use of the word presbyter for the second order of the ministry, despite the title, "The Ordination of Presbyters also called Priests". Presbyter is the New Testament word, the word, whether in Greek or Latin, for the second order throughout the liturgies of the East and West; but fundamentally what matters is the language of the ordination prayers, and it is impossible to maintain that this liturgy is less Catholic in its language than that of 1662: the truth is that it is more so. It is indeed a remarkable document and merits the closest study.

11

The Future of Prayer Book Revision

THE retention at the Reformation of liturgical worship, and in particular of the fixed rite of Holy Communion, in the Church of England has been one of the determining factors in her history. It is the common heritage of Prayer Book worship which has bound together through four centuries the different schools of thought which in every age have made up the Church of England. It is still loyalty to the Prayer Book, or at least general assent to it, which holds together those who theologically are widely sundered. And if we ask why this should be, the answer is the comparative simplicity of the Book, and its fidelity to the fundamental doctrines of the faith which the Creeds express. The average English churchman would rest content with the words of the 1662 Revisers: "We are fully persuaded in our judgments that the Book ... doth not contain in it anything contrary to the Word of God, or to sound doctrine, or which a godly man may not, with a good conscience, use and submit unto, or which is not fairly defensible against any that shall oppose the same." But the Prayer Book has not only been the bond of union in the Church; it has, under God, been instrumental in carrying it through periods of danger with its faith preserved. The strength of liturgy is that when securely based upon the Biblical revelation it ensures that worship shall be "in truth". The preached word may vary according to the doctrinal idiosyncrasies of the preacher; extempore prayer, both in its range and in its depth, is similarly conditioned, but a liturgy which is itself sound is a bastion against both false and shallow doctrine. This can be well illustrated from the history of English Christianity in the last three hundred years. The Puritan rejection of liturgy meant the decay of much of English Presbyterianism into Unitarianism in the eighteenth century and laid churches open to the dangers of a reduced Christology and a defective doctrine of Atonement in the late nineteenth century. It would not be fair to suggest that the Anglican Church passed through these periods unscathed. What is true is that as long as the Prayer Book was used the witness to the truth remained in Collects and Lections, and, most clearly of all, in the Holy Communion service. If the Cross of Christ is not preached from the pulpit there is still hope for a Church which enshrines it in her liturgy and makes that liturgy central in her life. This is only one side of the truth. Liturgy can never be a substitute for the ministry of the Word, but it can preserve the seeds of new life, and bear its testimony when preaching has become spiritually dead; and at every revival of spiritual life English church-men have found afresh in the Prayer Book worship the satisfaction of their needs and the sustenance of their new-found life. That was true of the Evangelical Revival and true of the Oxford movement.

The debt which the English Church owes to the makers of the Prayer Book is therefore immense; but, as what was said in Chapter 6 makes clear, we now have to face a new era in the history of Anglican worship, and one of much confusion. The crucial issues are theological and the theological climate has changed rapidly since the war. When *Prayer Book Revision in the Church of England* was written, preparatory to the Lambeth Conference of 1958, it could be said: "In 1928 many of the changes proposed in the Prayer Book were determined by the contemporary trends of thought rather than by genuinely biblical criteria. Thus the revival in biblical theology was bound to lead to a criticism of the 1928 Prayer Book." But since 1958 perhaps the most significant changes in theological thinking have been far more radical and, so far from being a continued growth of biblical theology, have so shifted the balance between divine transcendence and immanence that in some writers the very concept of the transcendence of God disappears. This is the issue of critical importance not only for theology but necessarily for Christian worship and prayer. It is with this in mind that all liturgical reconstruction must be judged. On the one hand it is true that worship must be relevant to the needs of men and the language of liturgy such that it can be an instrument of the Holy Spirit to communicate the faith. In that sense it must be contemporary. But it matters all the world that the concern for men which it embodies is God's concern seen in Jesus Christ our Lord. Charles Smyth's sentence, "The palmary criteria of liturgy are whether it makes sense and whether that sense accords with Holy Scripture", remains true, for our contemporary theological trends may be no more true than Gnosticism in the second century or Deism in the eighteenth.

Bound up with this same theological question is the survival of the Daily Office, the Anglican form of the *Opus Dei*. There are those who say simply that there is no need for it in the modern world and, in practice, abandon it. The whole question is well discussed by a Free Churchman, S. F. Winward, in *The Daily Office*, a report of the Joint Liturgical Group, in which he writes

The office is objective. It is theocentric. Its primary purpose is to offer praise to the "one God and Father of us all", who is above all and through all and in all. The Shorter Catechism compiled by the Westminster Assembly in 1647 opens with the well-known Question and Answer, "What is the chief end of Man? Man's chief end is to glorify God and to enjoy him for ever." The office is a means to the realisation of that end—the offering up of disinterested praise to the transcendent God. For this reason also, the basis of the office is the orderly reading of the Scriptures and the recitation of psalms.

Winward's whole essay deserves to be read by Anglicans, who from it can learn the value of their own heritage. But the passage quoted pinpoints both the theological and the practical issue. It is the loss of the sense of God's transcendence which makes the language of praise and adoration—and, therefore, much of the language both of the Psalms and the New Testament—meaningless. It may be admitted that worship is more difficult in solitude, even if it is recognized that all worship is with angels and archangels and all the company of heaven. It makes a real difference if only two or three are gathered in Christ's name. It may be true that we ask too much of this generation in the length of the Psalms and the lessons; and, as we have seen, proposals have been made to shorten them and to provide more variety in hymns and canticles. New translations of the Psalter (1963) and new versions of the Bible may help, but until we learn afresh the meaning of worship as the offering of disinterested praise to the transcendent God liturgical revision will itself avail little.

What is also true of the twentieth century is our realization of the importance for the Christian religion of what Canon Max Warren has called "the personalized corporate" in distinction from the mass society. It is this realization which has drawn together Evangelicals and Catholic-minded churchmen, and to its growth biblical theology has made no small contribution. This indeed is an essential part of the Liturgical Movement by which all the churches have been influenced. It is this new sense of the Church which makes nineteenth-century individualism so dated, so that today a phrase like "making my communion" is seldom heard, and it is taken for granted that communion is what we share. But the liturgical application of this insight, reinforced as it is by recent biblical studies, is much wider. The Church of Rome now teaches clearly that consecration is the act of the whole people of God and the priest their representative. And amongst Anglicans there is much wider agreement that when our Lord said "Do this in remembrance of me", or "for my memorial", he refers to the whole eucharistic action of blessing, breaking, and giving. Yet Jewel could write, and this is typical of Elizabethan Anglican teaching: "We ought to do that which Christ both did himself and also commanded us to do: and was afterwards practised in the apostles and holy fathers. He said thus, "Do ye this—that is, take ye bread, bless it, break it: give it in remembrance". We are reminded that in the 1552 Prayer Book the Words of Institution were followed immediately by "Take and eat this in remembrance". Here, and in Jewel, remembrance primarily applies to the act of receiving communion. The acceptance of the rite of 1967, even if some churchmen are a little unhappy, witnesses to the recognition that the whole eucharistic action is "in remembrance", a complete act. This does not mean that all differences between churchmen in their eucharistic theology are now at an end. Even though no responsible theologians of any communion maintain that the Eucharist can be a sacrifice additional to that of Calvary, there is still responsible opposition to the idea that we can offer Christ, or even offer his death or his passion. Hence the refusal of the House of Laity to accept the very primitive phrase "we offer this bread and this cup", even when that was understood as "offering the anamnesis of his passion". For this seemed to imply that anamnesis is a Godward action. Much biblical study—by Jeremias and Max Thurian, for example—would insist that this is the biblical meaning of the word, but Thurian's arguments are not accepted by Professor Douglas Jones or Professor C. F. D. Moule. The wording accepted in 1967, "With this bread and this cup we make the memorial" etc., leaves open the question whether anamnesis looks Godward or manward and can be interpreted as the pleading of our Lord's saving work. Probably this is as near as we can get to a form of words which is not divisive.

There are still, however, two other important questions requiring decision, both concerned with language. The first was raised by the Catechism Commission, who, as we have seen, felt it right to modernize the language considerably and with "a greater liberty than they would have felt had they been revising a part of the liturgy of the Church". Yet they say: "It has not been possible, nor would it be desirable, to avoid using certain terms which belong to the technical language of theology. No one can enter into the heritage of Christian faith and worship without some understanding of these words, and in our view it is part of the responsibility of the catechist to explain them." This states the liturgist's problem for him. Liturgy inevitably uses the great words of the Bible. However great the effort to be simple, the biblical background must be presupposed, and constant periphrasis becomes intolerable in the language of worship. An age which can "take" Shakespeare, or the technical language of the sciences, ought to be able to learn the great words of the Christian religion. But this means that the language of worship must be taught, and such teaching is the work of the Christian ministry.

The other widespread demand is that the language of the liturgy should be that of our own day; a demand voiced by many at the liturgical conference of 1966. What the Liturgical Commission tried to produce was language comparable to that of the Revised Standard Version of the Bible. Having taken advice from English scholars they purposely retained the address to God in the second person singular—thou and thee—which is also the use of the New English Bible. This, incidentally, enables the continued use of Cranmer's translation of the Collects with their beauty both of language and of rhythm. In a modern idiom which discards the vocative and addresses God as you, it would be imperative to rewrite them and do away with their relative clauses. For many churchmen this would be a grievous loss. Nevertheless the service for Baptism and Confirmation in a completely modern idiom, and modern translations of the Lord's Prayer, the Creeds, and the Canticles, were published by the Liturgical Commission in 1968[1] together with a text of the 1967 liturgy by one of its members. These may well influence liturgical changes when the present period of experiment comes to an end.

[1] *Modern Liturgical Texts*. S.P.C.K.

PART THREE

NOTES

1. *The early Liturgies*

In the first three centuries of Christendom the various local Churches developed their own liturgical form of the Holy Communion service. Liturgists in recent years have both traced the differences between local traditions and emphasized the pattern common to them all. When persecution ceased in the fourth century the differences began to disappear as lesser churches conformed their rites to those of the Patriarchal Sees. Antioch and Alexandria in the East and Rome in the West provide us with liturgies typical of their "spheres of influence" and these in turn react on one another. With the break up of the Roman Empire the different conditions of Eastern and Western Christendom affect the liturgical development. In the East Byzantium became politically dominant and the Byzantine liturgy, itself mainly derived from Antioch, suppressed the older rites even in the great sees. In the West where the barbarian invasions destroyed the unity of the Empire, the dominance of the Roman rite was delayed until unity was once more achieved under Charlemagne, and meanwhile the non-Roman rites of the West developed independently. We thus find two main types of liturgy in the West, the Italian, of which the Roman rite is ultimately the most important, and the Gallican itself subdivided into French and Spanish types. The main "families" of liturgy can now be set out.

I. Eastern

1. The Syrian rite: The Liturgy of St James. This is closely connected with Jerusalem, was adopted by Antioch in the fifth century, and eventually superseded by the Byzantine. The more ancient Antiochene rite is known to us in the writings of St John Chrysostom and in the Clementine liturgy of the Apostolic Constitutions.

2. The East Syrian rite: The Liturgy of SS. Addai and Mari, the ancient liturgy of the Church of Edessa. This has a history of its own, is Semitic not Greek, and addresses its consecration prayer to our Lord himself.

3. The Byzantine rite, the form finally dominant, in its two forms, the Liturgy of St Basil derived from Asia Minor and the Liturgy of St Chrysostom which is Antiochene in type. It was from this Byzantine rite (St Basil) that the *Epiklesis* of the 1549 book was in conception, derived.

II. The Egyptian Rite

This in its early stage is represented by the Liturgy of Sarapion (c. 340) and the ancient Alexandrian liturgy of St Mark. Its descendants are the Greek Liturgy of St Mark, the Coptic Liturgy and those of Abyssinia.

III. The Western Rites

1. The Italian rites chiefly represented by Rome and Milan. Behind them lies the Apostolic Tradition of Hippolytus. Though it has undergone considerable revision, the Roman rite preserves genuinely primitive elements. The symbolic language of its canon, markedly in contrast with the *metabolism* of the East, is a witness to primitive Eucharistic doctrine.

2. The Gallican rites, originally the local rites of France and Spain survive only in the Mozarabic rite of Toledo. Elsewhere they were suppressed and superseded by the Roman rite. Their chief characteristics are that almost all parts of the service, including the Eucharistic Prayer, vary with the Calendar, and the prayers lack the Roman austerity.

These rites coalesced, the Gallican influencing the Roman, so that our English liturgy is essentially a revision of a Romano-Gallican rite. Essentially it is a rite of the Reformation, the liturgical expression of the re-discovery by the Reformers of the meaning of Justification by faith. By that criterion it stands or falls.

2. The Daily Offices of the Sarum Breviary

Only such details are given as help in the understanding of the relationship of Morning and Evening Prayer to the medieval services. These were, Mattins, Lauds, Prime, Terce, Sext, None, Vespers, and Compline. Of these Mattins stands alone, the ancient night office in which the Bible reading was concentrated. Lauds and Vespers follow one model, Prime and Compline are structurally similar, and so are the Little Hours. The Prayer Book derivatives are italicized.

MATTINS consisted of *The Lord's Prayer* (said privately), *Versicles and Responses*, *Venite*, hymn, *Psalms* said in course with their antiphons, three *Lessons* (on Sundays and Festivals nine) and, on Festivals *Te Deum*.

LAUDS and VESPERS each had five *Psalms* (or Canticles) but only those for Vespers were said in course. These were followed by the office hymn, the Gospel Canticles, *Benedictus* (Lauds), and *Magnificat* (Vespers), Suffrages and Collect.

PRIME and COMPLINE each had fixed Psalms, an office hymn

(varied at Compline but not at Prime), the Canticles, Athanasian Creed (Prime) and *Nunc Dimittis* (Compline), suffrages, including at Prime *the Creed and Lord's Prayer*, and Collect.

TERCE, SEXT, NONE divided Psalm 119 between them, and beside a fixed hymn had varying Chapter and a Collect.

From this abbreviated outline, which omits details like the Capitulum, it can be seen how Morning Prayer is built up from Mattins, Lauds, and Prime, and Evening Prayer from Vespers and Compline.

3. *The Black Rubric*

This was first inserted in 1552 when the second Prayer Book had already been sent to the printers and is so called because of the heavy type in which it was set. It was the result of an attempt by John Knox to introduce, despite Cranmer's protest, the Swiss custom of sitting to receive communion. The Council, on its own authority, ordered its insertion into the Prayer Book in order to make it clear that kneeling does not imply "that any adoration is done, or ought to be done, either unto the sacramental bread or wine where bodily received, or unto any real and essential presence there being of Christ's natural flesh and blood." This declaration on kneeling was signed by the King but not passed by the Convocations and was omitted in 1559. It was restored in a revised form at the request of the Puritans at the Savoy Conference, with the change of "real and essential" into "corporal". "Real" in the sixteenth century meant presence *in re* or *realiter*. Jewel, using "real" in this sense, equates "real" and "corporal". But by the seventeenth century the word "real" was acquiring its modern sense of genuine and no longer meant presence in or after the manner of a thing. The Caroline divines were deeply concerned to insist that Christ's spiritual presence is real in the modern sense of the word, and they therefore omitted the word from the rubric, denying only a corporal presence. Cosin's own words may be quoted. "The body and blood is neither sensibly present—nor otherwise at all present but only to them that are duly prepared to receive them, and in the very act of receiving them and the consecrated elements together, to which they are sacramentally in that act united."[1]

4. *The Homilies*

The Homilies are important as illustrating the doctrinal position of the Reformers. They are prescribed in the Prayer Book as an alternative to the sermon, and Article 35 refers to them as "Godly and

[1] Cosin, *Works*, V. 345, quoted by J. T. Tomlinson in *The Prayer Book, Articles and Homilies*, p. 177.

wholesome doctrine". There are two books of quite different date and character. The first book was published in 1547 and contains twelve sermons, four of them including the great homily on salvation, by Cranmer. Such a work had been proposed by Convocation as early as 1542, and some of the sermons were so far unreformed as to be re-published with but little change in Mary's reign. The later ones were designed to teach the doctrine implied by the Prayer Book services. The second book was, except for the last homily, completed in 1563, and authorized in 1571. It contains twenty-one sermons, is much more Calvinist in tone, and one of its chief contributors was Bishop Jewel. What is interesting is the constant appeal of the Homilies not only to Holy Scripture but to the early Fathers.

INDEX

Index

Agapé 15
Alcuin 30
Ambrose, St 23, 30, 85
Andrewes, Bp 66
Apostolic Constitutions 9, 14, 23, 30
Apostolic Tradition 13, 16, 20, 22, 111
Articles of Religion 41f, 48
Augustine, St 11, 34

Baptism 20–2, 54, 97ff, 101–5
Benedict, St 23
Bible 35, 37, 43, 84, 90
Bidding of the Bedes 88
Black Rubric 129
Breviary 26f, 45, 128
Bucer 39, 46, 54, 98
Burial of the Dead 33f, 108f

Calendar 50
Calvin 10, 11, 46, 47
Canticles 84f
Catechumenate 13, 21
Ceremonies 49f
Christian year 8, 24
Chrysostom 32; Prayer of 91
Clement of Rome 13
Collects 67, 89ff
Commandments 53, 66
Communion Table 66
Confession and Absolution 72, 105ff
Confirmation 22, 100ff
Consecration Prayer 16ff, 73ff, 77, 80
Cranmer, Abp 35ff, 51ff, 90
Creed 18, 21, 48, 51, 67, 79, 84, 87
Cyprian 13, 16, 30

Daily Offices 22–4, 29, 51, 82–92
Didaché 13, 14, 20
Duchesne 17n, 114

Eastward Position 19, 66, 74
Egyptian Church Order 13
Epiklesis 9, 16, 74, 77
Epistle 67

Freeman 23

Gallican rites 25f, 113, 128
Gardiner, Bp 40, 52
Gloria in Excelsis 53, 66, 76, 79, 85, 86
Gospel 17, 67
Gregory the Great 23, 32, 34

Hermann's *Consultation* 46, 72, 93, 98, 100, 108
Hippolytus 13, 14, 16, 22
Holy Communion 6, 31, 44, 65–81
Homilies 68, 129

Intercession (the great) 13, 17, 70f, 77, 79
Invocation of Saints 37, 38, 40, 51, 90, 93

Justin Martyr 13, 15, 20, 68

Kyrie 17, 32, 53, 66, 77, 79

Latin (services in) 26f
Litany 32f, 37, 79, 92ff
Liturgical Revision: Reformation, 35ff; seventeenth century, 47, 54f; twentieth century, 56ff, 76–81, 91f, 95f, 101f, 116f; future, 119ff

Liturgies 13–19, 127f
Liturgy (principle of) 6–8, 24, 90, 119
Luther 45f

Manual 27
Manual acts 66
Marriage 33, 107f
Mass 28–31, 44, 65
Merbecke 68
Missal 27

Oblation 10, 16, 30, 40, 42, 74f, 77, 80
Occasional Offices 97–109
Offertory 69f
Ordinal 38, 53, 94–100, 110–18

Pliny 13, 15
Prayer (types of) 88
Prayer Books: 1549—37f, 48–52;
    1552—39–41, 53f, 77–9; 1928—53,
    67, 70–3, 77, 79, 85f, 88f, 94, 98,
    106, 109
Priesthood 12, 44, 111ff, 115, 118
Primer 28, 34
Processional 27, 32
Proper (of the Mass) 24, 67
Proper Prefaces 73, 80
Proper Psalms 84
Psalms 14, 23, 26, 43, 50, 84–6
Puritans 47, 54f, 83, 116

Quicunque 85f
Quiñon, Cardinal 45

Reformation 35ff; Continental 45–8
Requiem 33, 109
Reservation 106f

Sacramentary 88
Sacraments 7ff
Sacrifice 6; of the Mass 30f, 42, 44,
    52, 65, 75, 122f
Sarapion, Bp 13
Sarum use 26
Savoy Conference 47
Scripture lections 15, 43, 50f, 67f, 86
Sermon 15, 17, 43, 68, 83, 119f
Service books 27f
Synagogue 14f, 23

Table prayers 71
Te Deum 45, 85f
Tertullian 13, 20, 30
Thanksgiving (1662 prayer of) 76
Tradition of the instruments 53, 113f

Unction 106

Vestments 50
Visitation of the sick 105ff

Worship 3–12

Zwingli 46